LEAVING CERTIFICATE

LESS STRESS MORE SUCCESS

Art History
Revision

Áine Ní Chárthaigh

g GILL EDUCATION

Gill Education
Hume Avenue
Park West
Dublin 12
www.gilleducation.ie

Gill Education is an imprint of M.H. Gill & Co.

ISBN: 978-0-7171-79305

Design: Liz White Designs
Illustrations: Keith Barrett and Áine Ní Chárthaigh

At the time of going to press, all web addresses were active and contained information relevant to the topics in this book. Gill Education does not, however, accept responsibility for the content or views contained on these websites. Content, views and addresses may change beyond the publisher or author's control. Students should always be supervised when reviewing websites.

For permission to reproduce photographs, the author and publisher gratefully acknowledge the following:

© akg-images: 103, © Alamy: 22C, 61, 70TCL, 70CR, 71CL, 71BR, 79TCL, 79TC, 79TR, 79BR, 82BL, 82BC, 89, 104, 114T, 114B, 177, 183; © Bridgeman Images: 122L, 122R, 128, 129, 130, 131, 133, 135T, 135B, 137, 138, 139T, 142, 143, 147, 153, 154, 155T, 155B, 158, 167T, 167B, 172, 175BL, 175BR, 181, 190; © Bridgeman Images / © Succession Picasso / DACS, London 2017: 209, 210, 211; Department of Environment, Heritage and Local Government: 79TL, 82BR, 87; © Getty Images: 23, 70TC, 79BL, 101, 112, 139B, 146, 151, 176, 186, 187; © iStock: 79TCR, 79BC; © Joe Caslin: 216; © National Gallery of Ireland: 156; National Monuments Service / Dept. of Arts, Heritage, Regional, Rural and Gaeltacht Affairs: 22B, 49T, 57T, 70TL, 70TCR, 70CL, 70BL, 70BR, 71TL, 71TR, 71CR, 71BL, 76; © National Museum of Ireland: 29, 35, 38, 39, 41, 42, 43, 44, 45, 47, 64, 66, 67, 69; Photo © State Hermitage Museum © Succession H. Matisse: 206; © Succession H. Matisse: 207; Wikimedia: 49B, 70TR, 119. Sketches on pp. 32, 33, 54, 55, 222–5 by Rory O'Driscoll; sketches on pp. 200, 202, 204 by Clodagh Fitton.

The paper used in this book is made from the wood pulp of managed forests. For every tree felled, at least one tree is planted, thereby renewing natural resources.

CONTENTS

Leaving Certificate Art

Art is an excellent choice for the Leaving Certificate. As a creative subject, it not only offers a space to reflect and breathe during the intensity of the Leaving Certificate years, it also provides an opportunity to see and interpret the world in a new way. Even mundane things can seem fresh and exciting when colour and shape awakens the imagination.

From 2018, Art will have an added advantage. Two of the practical components will be assessed as one unit, and this work will be generated entirely within normal class time over a period of 10 weeks. This means that exactly half of the Art examination is free from highly pressurised conditions.

Art as a Leaving Certificate subject can also prove highly valuable in later careers. The role of Art in creative problem-solving has long been identified as an essential tool to help solve issues for which there is no single, clear solution. Many employers seek people with an innovative approach, and this is exactly what artists – or those with artistic styles of thinking – can provide.

key point

You must take Art as a school-based subject.

Due to revised assessment arrangements, it is not possible for a student taking Art on their own or with private tuition outside of a school or centre to meet with authentication requirements. Therefore, the State Examinations Commission cannot accept coursework from such candidates.

Art as a career

Art, of course, continues to be an option for students wishing to pursue 'traditional' creative careers, such as Architecture, Interior Design or Painting-/Fine Art-related professions, but the emergence of the internet has provided a new and very practical reason to study Art, generating as it has an abundance of exciting new roles.

With the proliferation of computers, smartphones, tablets and other portable electronic devices, there are increased opportunities for digital designers and multimedia artists.

key point

Most businesses have an online presence, leading not only to more demand for web designers but for app designers, software designers, graphic designers, digital illustrators, multimedia artists, video producers, animators and game designers.

Film

The Irish film industry has grown hugely over the last decade, and is now estimated to be worth over €550 million. Among the 6,000 individuals and 500 businesses employed directly and indirectly, there are numerous Art-related opportunities. In recent years, two Art-based animated Irish films, *The Secret of Kells* and *Song of the Sea*, were nominated for Best Animated Feature at the Oscars.

Exam format

PAPER	EXAM DURATION (HOURS)	TIME OF YEAR	MARKS ALLOWED	PERCENTAGE OF THE EXAM
Practical Coursework Craftwork/Design and Imaginative Composition/Still Life	30 hours of class time	Jan–Apr	200	50%
Life Sketching	1 hour	May	50	12.5%
History and Appreciation of Art (3 essays, each worth 50 marks)	2½ hours	May	150	37.5%

Revised assessment for Practical Components 2018

Two of the four examination components for Leaving Certificate Art, which were previously carried out as invigilated examinations, will instead be carried out as a single coursework component in the examination of 2018 and afterwards.

Imaginative Composition or **Still Life** and **Craftwork** or **Design**

will be executed as coursework in schools over an extended period of time.

If you have ability in Art and love the subject, don't be convinced to give it up in favour of a more 'useful' subject – unless, of course, you want to. Remember, a high grade is impressive in any subject, and because Art enhances fine motor skills, hand–eye coordination, problem-solving skills, lateral thinking, complex analysis and critical thinking skills, it will stand to you in any career.

Practical Coursework

Craftwork or Design and Imaginative Composition or Still Life

The completed coursework component submitted for assessment must consist of **two** realised works from the Leaving Certificate Art Coursework Brief and **a record of their development** in the Coursework Workbook. Your investigation and development based on your chosen theme must be recorded in your Coursework Workbook using the prescribed structure.

The coursework component you submit for assessment must be **your own individual work**. To enable your **Art teacher** to validate your coursework component and to ensure that similar constraints apply to all candidates, the workbook and realised works in their entirety must be executed in school under the supervision of your class teacher.

The use of primary sources is required (you must work from real objects, not pictures). Primary sources are sources, physical or conceptual, that are viewed in their original state and are not filtered through another person's interpretation of them. You may use a combination of physical and conceptual sources (working from imagination, memory or feeling).

Practical Coursework links

To watch a short video on the Art student's experience, go to YouTube and search for 'PDST ART STUDENT EXPERIENCE' (2:59).

To see the work of some exceptional Art students from all over the world, visit www.studentartguide.com/featured

Life Sketching

- Drawing from the human figure.
- A standing pose is completed in 15 minutes and a longer pose in 30 minutes.
- Students must draw the full figure and it may be completed in any medium.

History and Appreciation of Art

The fields of special study covered by the exam are as follows:

- **Section I**: Art in Ireland (from prehistoric times to the present).
- **Section II**: European Art (from AD 1000 to the present).
- **Section III**: General Appreciation topics based on everyday visual experience.

The History and Appreciation of Art paper offers a choice of topics and will include one from each special study area. You will be asked for three fully illustrated, essay-style answers, one from each of the three sections of the paper. Each essay carries equal marks.

History and Appreciation of Art

The Art History syllabus is extremely broad and general. The style and content of the exam has changed over the years, but questions are framed to test quite detailed knowledge, especially at Higher Level.

Section I Art in Ireland and Section II European Art require factual knowledge. Section III General Appreciation requires a more general level of artistic awareness, but even in this section the questions can be quite specific.

Preparing for the History and Appreciation of Art exam paper

You should:

- Study your chosen sections in as much detail as possible.
- Carefully examine past papers and marking schemes.
- Practise answering questions from past papers.

The exam paper has determined the History of Art syllabus for some time, so study past exam questions from the previous five or six years very carefully. Check the marking scheme to help you study in a more focused way.

- Use the internet for full-size coloured images and extra information.
- Visit museums and galleries whenever possible so that you can see the original works.

Study areas

Choose your study areas from the following:

Section I: Art in Ireland

Study at least **one** area in detail and have a good outline knowledge of another.

1. Pre-Christian Ireland
- The Stone Age.
- The Bronze Age: Early, Middle and Late.
- The Iron Age/Celtic/La Tène era.

2. Early Christian Ireland
- Architecture.
- Manuscripts.
- Metalwork.
- Stone carving/High Crosses.

3. Georgian Ireland
- Palladian architecture and decorative arts.
- Neoclassical architecture and decorative arts.

Section II: European Art

Choose at least **one** area to study in detail.

4. Medieval Europe
- Romanesque architecture and sculpture.
- Gothic architecture and sculpture.
- Gothic stained glass.
- Fourteenth-century Gothic architecture.
- Fourteenth-century Gothic painting and sculpture.
- Painting in Italy: Giotto.

5. The Renaissance
- Painting: Early and High.
- Sculpture: Early and High.
- Architecture.
- Renaissance in Venice.
- Renaissance in Northern Europe.

6. Impressionism and twentieth-century art movements

- Painting in nineteenth-century France.
- Modern European art movements.
- Individual artists associated with nineteenth- and twentieth-century art movements.

Section III: General Appreciation

Topics vary considerably, but some topics appear regularly. Some of these can be studied (e.g. film and design), while others depend more on a general awareness of visual surroundings.

- Museum and gallery visits.
- Film studies.
- Roadside and public sculpture.
- The built environment.
- Graphic design, interior design and product design.
- General topics relating to visual appreciation.

Revision plans

WEEK	LESSON 1 (1 HOUR) SAT: 10AM–11AM • READ BOOK • RESEARCH INTERNET • MAKE NOTES • PLAN ESSAYS FROM EXAM PAPERS	LESSON 2 (30 MINS) TUES: 5PM–5.30PM • READ BOOK • READ OVER PREVIOUS ESSAYS AND HOMEWORK	LESSON 3 (30 MINS) THURS: 9PM–9.30PM • DRAW
WEEK 1 2 DEC	THE STONE AGE STONE MONUMENTS	BACKGROUND LIFESTYLE HOUSING	TOMBS PATTERNS ON STONES
WEEK 2 9 DEC	BRONZE AGE PERIODS ORNAMENTS METHODS OF DECORATION	BACKGROUND LIFESTYLE MINING ALLUVIAL	ORNAMENTS DECORATION
WEEK 3 16 DEC	LA TÈNE: THE CELTS & IRON AGE CULTURE LA TÈNE: ART MOTIFS	LA TÈNE ORNAMENTS	ORNAMENTS STONE DETAIL
WEEK 4 6 JAN	PUBLIC SCULPTURE AND THE BUILT ENVIRONMENT	READ OVER PAST APPRECIATION QUESTIONS	DIAGRAMS OBJECTS PAINTING SCULPTURE
WEEK 5 13 JAN	ROMANESQUE ARCHITECTURE CHARACTERISTICS	MEDIEVAL EUROPE THE CHURCH & SOCIETY PILGRIMAGES	ROMANESQUE VAULTS PLAN OF PILGRIMAGE CHURCH

WEEK 6 20 JAN	ROMANESQUE SCULPTURE TYMPANUM: AUTUN & VÉZELAY	ROMANESQUE ART THEMES & STYLE	SCULPTURE FROM AUTUN & VÉZELAY
WEEK 7 27 JAN	GOTHIC ARCHITECTURE CHARACTERISTICS COMPARISON TO ROMANESQUE	ORIGINS OF GOTHIC GOTHIC CATHEDRALS PURPOSE OF GOTHIC ART	RIB VAULTING FLYING BUTTRESS
WEEK 8 3 FEB	GOTHIC SCULPTURE SCULPTURE & ARCHITECTURE CHARTRES, REIMS, NOTRE DAME PARIS	COLUMN STATUES THE SAINTS IN ART	COLUMN STATUES FIGURES FROM THE DOORS
WEEK 9 10 FEB	STAINED GLASS FOURTEENTH-CENTURY SCULPTURE	CHARTRES CATHEDRAL SAINT CHAPELLE	THE BLUE VIRGIN OF CHARTRES
WEEK 10 17 FEB	PAINTING: INTER-NATIONAL STYLE	DUC DE BERRY WILTON DIPTYCH	WILTON DIPTYCH DUC DE BERRY

Work out your time per week and the material you need to cover. These sample plans may help you coming up to the Pre-Leaving Cert in early spring. Use a similar method to plan again for the exam in June.

Planning and writing an Art History or Appreciation essay

1. **Read the question carefully.**
2. **Highlight** key words that identify the **task** and indicate what needs to be done, e.g. 'describe', 'discuss'.
3. **Examine** the dictionary meaning of the word **discuss**: to consider or examine by argument; to talk over or write about.
4. **Identify** the **topic words** that indicate the subject of the essay, e.g. Bronze Age.
5. **Study** the subject in your textbook and do some background research from internet sources.
6. **Make** written notes on important facts and relevant art terms.
7. **Plan** a response to the statement.
8. **Highlight** important points of your discussion. This will form the backbone of the essay. It will be stated in the introduction but it also needs to be restated with reference to named artworks.
9. **Select** facts related to the topic from your textbook and make sure these are relevant to the question.

10. **Check** your facts by asking: **What? Where? When? How? Why?** and **Why do you think?**

11. **Sketches:** Practise sketching the artefacts and artworks – you will learn a great deal by drawing and selecting suitable information for annotations.

Writing style

Use the essay writing skills you have developed for Leaving Certificate English (or Irish) as a basis, but remember:

- In Art History, the most important element is the interpretation of the question and the factual information you choose to support this.

Marks are awarded for:

- Facts and discussion of facts.
- Analysis of artworks.

Writing style options include:

- Traditional-style essay, involving an introduction, several paragraphs and a conclusion.
- A combination of bullet points and paragraphs.
- A series of well-developed points and annotated sketches that convey relevant detailed information.

key point

Make your essay special!
Textbooks are designed to give you the facts, but your essay should also reflect your individual response to artists and artworks. It should be written in a special and colourful language – yours!

Past exam questions

- Visit www.examinations.ie, which contains an examination material archive for past papers and marking schemes.
- Examine past papers. As a general rule, questions will follow a similar format every year.
- Examine marking schemes. These vary from question to question and year to year, but they can really help to break down the question and focus where to place emphasis in your answer.

Ordinary Level example questions

Planning your answer

- Look carefully at the illustration. Describe what you see.
- Write as clearly as you can.
- Use headings in different colours if you like.
- Use bullet points or paragraphs.
- Make good sketches and add notes to these.

key point

Have the confidence to put forward your individual response to an artwork. Your essay will be all the more interesting for it. In other words: if you like it, say so and say why!

Section I: Art in Ireland – Question 1 (2016)

The Gleninsheen Gorget, illustrated on the accompanying sheet [see page 42] is an example of Irish metalwork from the Bronze Age.

Answer (a), (b) and (c).

(a) What was its function?

(b) Describe and discuss how this object was made and decorated.

(c) Name and briefly describe and discuss one other artefact from the Bronze Age.

Illustrate your answer.

Marking scheme

Q. 1		Marks	Notes
A	Function	**10**	
B	Description and discussion of how it was made and decorated	**20**	
C	Name, description and discussion of one other piece of Bronze Age metalwork	**15**	5 for name 10 for discussion
D	Sketches	**5**	
	Total	**50**	

Break down the question

A. **Describe** the Gleninsheen Gorget as you see it in the illustration. Give as many facts as you can about **this object only!**

   What was it for? Who might wear it? Add your own opinion here.

   How was it made and decorated?

B. Give as many facts about its making and decorating as you can.

   Explain the decoration methods – repoussé and incision.

C. **Choose another object, e.g. the Gold Lunula**
   - Why was it called this name?
   - Who might have worn it and why?
   - How was it made and decorated?
   - Was it Early, Middle or Late Bronze Age?

D. **2 sketches:**
   - The Gold Lunula.
   - Detail of the decoration on the narrow end.

Section II: European Art – Question 8 (2016)

The Last Judgement by Gislebertus is illustrated on the accompanying sheet [see page 103].
Answer (a) and (b).

(a) Describe and discuss the illustration under the following headings:

- Subject matter
- Composition
- Function

(b) Briefly describe and discuss the main features of a Romanesque church or cathedral.

Illustrate your answer.

Marking scheme

Q. 8		Marks
A	Description and discussion of the illustration under headings	30
B	Description and discussion of the main features of a Romanesque church	15
C	Sketches	5
	Total	50

Break down the question

Thirty marks are allocated for the description and discussion of this very famous scene. Take your time and examine it in detail. Describe what you see:

A. **Subject matter:** What is this scene about? Describe what is happening on both sides. Who are the figures? Do you find them interesting? Why?

   Composition: What shape is the scene? How are the figure groups arranged? What separates the different groups?

   Function: Why was this scene made? Who visited the church? How do you think people would have been affected by the artwork at that time?

B. **The important features of a Romanesque church**

- How did they look?
- How were they built?
- How was the building designed to cater for the needs of visitors? Show this in a plan.
- What were the roofs made of? How were they held up? Show this in a sketch.

C. **Sketches – add notes**

- A plan of a Romanesque church.
- Romanesque vaulting.

Section III: Appreciation – Question 10 (2016)

A public park is an area of land reserved for the enjoyment and recreation of visitors.

Answer (a) and (b).

(a) Design and discuss a layout for a public park to include the following amenities:

- Family picnic area
- Toddlers' play area
- Dog walking trail

(b) Choose one of the amenities above and outline the health and safety features that this area would require. Give reasons for your choices.

Illustrate your answer.

Marking scheme

Q. 10		Marks
A	Design/plan of park with amenities	20
B	Description and discussion of health and safety features of chosen amenity	20
C	Sketches	10
	Total	50

Break down the question

This is a very open question and is a great opportunity for you to explore your own thoughts and ideas. Try basing your thoughts on a park near you, one you might have visited or seen on TV. Imagine what you would like to have in your area. A lot of your ideas can be shown in drawings; add notes to explain what you mean.

A. **Imagine where the park is located.** Is it near a river? In a busy city centre or part of a town or village? Is it near the sea? Is there a wooded area? Is there a lake or pond?

- **Draw a plan** of the areas – add in diagrams to show grass, paths and flowers, as well as the picnic areas, toddlers' play area and the dog walking trail.
- **Describe your ideas** for the picnic area – the tables, seating, shelter, grass for sitting on, etc. Is the area safe for children? How would you make it safe?
- **Drawing 1: The picnic area – add notes**

B. **Describe your ideas** for the toddlers' play area. Is it near the picnic area? What would small children like to do best?

- **Drawing 2: The play area – add notes**
- **Describe your ideas** for the dog walking path. Is it well away from the picnic area and the toddlers' area? Can two people pass easily? How long should it be? Is it along a river or through a wooded area?

- **What measures** in the playground would you suggest so that small children can run, hide and climb safely? **How** would you prevent them from running off?
- **How** would you stop them finding dangerous or dirty things?

Higher Level example questions

Section I: Art in Ireland – Question 1 (2016)

'By developing skills of working in gold, Bronze Age artists and craftworkers ushered in a new period of cultural development in Ireland.'

Discuss this statement with reference to **two** named artefacts from this period. In your answer describe and discuss form, function, materials used and decorative techniques.

and

Briefly describe and discuss where and how Bronze Age people in Ireland acquired the metals needed for their artefacts.

Illustrate your answer.

Marking scheme

Q. 1		Marks	Notes
A	Discussion of statement and two named artefacts from this period	10	5 for discussion of statement 3/2 for names
B	Description and discussion of named artefact 1 under form, function, materials used and decorative techniques	10	
C	Description and discussion of named artefact 2 under form, function, materials used and decorative techniques	10	
D	Briefly describe and discuss where and how Bronze Age people acquired the metals needed	10	2 examples and information
E	Sketches	10	
	Total	**50**	

Break down the question

You have been asked to **discuss two artefacts. This means that** only **5 marks** are allowed for the initial discussion. Include the named artefacts in the initial discussion and discuss them in detail later.

- 10 marks each is allocated for the discussion and description of these artefacts.
- A further 10 marks is allocated for information and discussion on metalworking in Ireland.

Instead of a long opening discussion, the main emphasis should focus on:

A. **Why** the developing skills of the artists and craftworkers ushered in a new period of culture and **how** the two **named** artefacts you have chosen show this.

   How craftwork skills developed over the period.

   What this tells us about society and cultural development.

B. **Why** artefact 1 (e.g. the Gleninsheen Gorget) is a good example of development of these skills. Using the given headings, describe how was it made and decorated. What was it used for?

C. **Why** artefact 2 (e.g. the Gorteenareagh Lock Rings) shows further development of the craftworkers' skills. Using the given headings, describe how they were made and decorated. What were they used for?

D. **Brief description** of how and why metalworking came to Ireland.

   What metals were used.

   Where was the raw ore found (two examples, e.g. bronze and gold).

   How this was mined.

E. **Sketches:** Include three sketches in the main body of the essay or at the end.

   Label and annotate (include notes).

   Use colour or black and white depending on which would convey the most relevant and supportive information.

See an example of the finished essay on page 16.

Section II: The Renaissance – Question 9 (2016)

'Donatello (1386–1466) was an artistic innovator who created dramatic works of art.'

Discuss this statement with reference to *Mary Magdalene*, illustrated on the accompanying sheet [see page 131]. In your answer refer to subject matter, composition, treatment of the human figure and the period in which this work was produced.

and

Name and briefly describe and discuss one other work by Donatello.

Illustrate your answer.

Marking scheme

Q. 9		Marks	Notes
A	Discussion of statement	10	
B	Discussion of *Mary Magdalene* with reference to subject matter and composition	10	
C	Discussion of *Mary Magdalene* with reference to treatment of the human figure and the period in which it was produced	10	
D	Name and brief description and discussion of one other work by Donatello	15	5 for name 10 for description & discussion
E	Sketches	5	
	Total	**50**	

Break down the question

The accompanying image on the exam paper helps you to describe the artwork but note that it also means only 5 marks for sketches.

Thirty marks are allocated to discussion of the statement with reference to the named and illustrated work. The response should therefore focus on:

A. **Why Donatello was an artistic innovator**

- Training, working techniques and motivation.
- A master in both marble and bronze.
- Brunelleschi's influence – proportion and perspective.
- Studies in Rome – classical influence.
- Studies from life – new at that time.

Why his work was so dramatic (e.g. *St Mark* and *St George* at Orsanmichele), lifelike and realistic – a complete departure from traditional sculpture.

- David – first-life sized nude; polished bronze.
- *Gattamelata*, the first equestrian statue since classical times – bronze a difficult medium; caused a sensation in its day.

Sketch with annotation, e.g. *David*

B. **Discussion**

Examination of the illustration. Refer to this as you describe, e.g. 'the illustration shows ... etc.'

- Why *Mary Magdalene* shows Donatello's artistic skills.
- Why it could be considered the most dramatic of all Donatello's works.

Subject matter: The character. A figure of sadness – use descriptive words and expressions like 'haunting', 'harrowing', 'a reminder of human tragedy'.

Composition: Tall and thin; a very long contrapposto pose (weight on one leg); head slightly tilted; shows the influence of classical sculpture.

C. **Treatment of the human figure:** Donatello's unique ability to create such a vibrant work of energy and power.

- Carved in wood and painted originally, the figure shows the effects of suffering and pain; is eaten up by fasting; hands lifted in prayer; long, bony fingers that do not touch; traces of colour; sad blue eyes, hollow sockets, broken teeth; covered in long, yellowed hair, matted and twisted around her body.
- Slightly bent over but still graceful – head held high.
- Lifelike, timeless and has the power to affect the emotions even today.

Period in which it was produced

- Early Renaissance Florence – a thriving centre of trade and culture with a high standard of living.
- Private patrons; guilds of Florence; members had humanist values; wanted the classical style for the sculpture of the city.
- The arts flourished but the artist's own ideas were rarely considered.

D. **A work by Donatello**, e.g. *The Feast of Herod*

- Describe by referring to subject – composition medium, the human figure.
- Why this is a good example of Donatello as innovator.
- Donatello's ability to convey emotion – compare to *Mary Magdalene*.

Sketch with annotation – *The Feast of Herod*

Artists and art movements

Look carefully at Questions 14 and 15 on the exam paper. These give a list of artworks and art movements.

- **Artworks by a named artist.** If you have studied a range of topics or visited an art museum, you may very well find you can ably answer a question on a particular artwork. Note, however, that you will always have to briefly describe and discuss **one other work** by the artist you have chosen.
- **Art style or movement.** As well as the characteristics of the movement, this question will also ask that you describe and discuss **one named work** by a **named artist** whose work is typical of this.

Appreciation questions that draw on skills from Practical Art class

Some Appreciation questions draw on skills from Practical Art class. For example, a question on a visit to an art gallery might also ask: how would you organise an art exhibition in your school? This gives you the opportunity to describe and draw something you are familiar with and excited about. It also has huge scope for imagination. Similarly, the following question on roadside sculpture allows you to draw on experience you may have gained with 3D, clay modelling or ceramics in school.

Section III: Appreciation of Art – Question 18 (2015)

'Site-specific sculpture on Irish roadsides gives the public an opportunity to view well-crafted contemporary works of art.'

Discuss this statement, referring to the images illustrated on the accompanying sheet. In your answer, refer to scale, materials and technique, colour/finish, context, and visual impact on the environment.

and

Briefly outline your ideas for a sculpture, which would enhance an outdoor space at your school. Give reasons for your design decisions.

Illustrate your answer.

Marking scheme

Q. 18		Marks
A	Discussion of statement	10
B	Discussion of the image illustrated, referring to scale, materials and technique, colour/finish, context and visual impact on the environment	20
C	Brief outline of your own ideas for a sculpture that would enhance an outdoor space at your school, giving reasons for your design decisions	15
D	Sketches	5
	Total	50

Break down the question

Notice that discussion is awarded 30 marks – 10 for the initial statement and a further 20 for your thoughts on the illustrated work using the given headings. Your own ideas and design proposal with sketches accounts for 20 marks.

Look at the illustration and discuss:

A. **Why do you think** this work offers such an opportunity to the public?

   Why is this a well-crafted contemporary work of art?

   Explain the term 'site-specific'.

B. **Describe** what you see – in scale, materials and technique, colour/finish, context.

   How do you think it impacts visually on the environment?

C. **Outline your ideas for a school sculpture:**

- **Why** you chose this theme.
- **How it** is designed – composition; shape; visual impact on the environment.
- **What is the** concept/idea of the work?
- **Why you think** this will suit the school?
- **Which** artworks inspired you?
- **What** material would you choose?
- **What** size would it be?
- **Who** would enjoy or benefit from this work?
- **Who** would make the finished piece?

D. **Sketch 1:** The sculpture in its setting – the school outdoor location, including notes and measurements.

Sketch 2: The sculpture – with notes on design; concept; materials and finish.

Higher Level example answer

Question 1 (2016) (See question and plan on page 11)

(A)

Gold was first seen in Ireland during the Bronze Age sometime between 2000 and 500 BC. We have very little detailed information on that society, but we do know that more gold objects were found here than any other European country, which suggests that society had become sophisticated and an upper class had probably developed. This is because gold has no real practical purpose, but its beautiful colour and rarity makes it highly desirable. Members of an 'aristocracy' would have wanted elaborate gold ornaments like the Gorteenareagh Lock Rings or the Gleninsheen Gorget to show their high status, especially on ceremonial occasions. They would have needed skilled artists and craftsmen who would have become more and more skilled over time as they worked hard to meet this demand, and the splendid gold ornaments they produced ushered in an entirely new period of cultural development.

Decorative gold objects

Early Bronze Age objects like the neck ornaments known as lunulae and discs of thin gold sheet were relatively simple. Methods of decoration included incision, cutting small lines on the surface and repoussé (hammering out the design from the back). As time went on, however, a variety of more sophisticated objects like torcs, waistbands and earrings were produced by elegantly twisting bars or thin strips of gold.

Sketch 1: *Repoussé and flange twisting.*

(B)

The Gleninsheen Gorget – Late Bronze Age, c. 600 BC

In the Late Bronze Age there was a huge upsurge in the production of gold ornaments like large solid dress fasteners and intricate hair rings. This took place somewhere between 1200–500 BC and has become known as Irelands first 'Golden Age'. The craft worker's techniques and decorative skills reached the highest standard known in Europe at the time. Of all the objects, the gorget is perhaps the most beautifully made. There are several gorgets in the National Museum, but the Gleninsheen Gorget, found in a rock crevice in the Burren in Co. Clare, is the most perfect of these.

Sketch 2: *The Gleninsheen Gorget*

Form

This is a U-shaped gold collar with a disc connected to each end.

Function

Gorgets are unique to Ireland, and these dramatic objects must have been worn by someone with a high status in society. They are large and quite heavy so would more likely have been worn only on ceremonial occasions on a man's chest rather than around the neck.

Material used

The gorget is made mainly from sheet gold. Gold is a soft material and is easily moulded into shape. This can be seen on the outer and inner edges of the collar, which were finished with a strip of gold wrapped around it to create a smooth finish.

Decorative techniques

The skilled artistry of the ancient craftworkers is especially evident in the decoration of the Gleninsheen Gorget. The body of the collar is woven into six rows of plain and very finely rope-patterned repoussé. This alternately smooth and textured pattern catches the light beautifully and gives the impression of movement.

The discs at either end were made from two layers. The technology of soldering was not yet known, so the inner disc was connected to the collar by stitching with gold wire and then covered with an outer disc. Once again, the edges of the larger inner disc were folded over to give a smooth edge.

The outer discs are patterned with little circles, each with concentric rings incised/cut into the surface (probably with a scalpel or a compass) surrounding a raised cone. Rows of beads in repoussé surround a larger inner circle and the edges of the discs.

Sketch 3: *Detail of the terminal – Gleninsheen Gorget*

(C)

The Gorteenareagh Lock Rings – Late Bronze Age, c. 600 BC

These lock or tress rings are some of the finest objects of the Late Bronze Age. It is not known whether they would have been worn by a man or a woman, but structurally these are the most advanced work of Irish goldsmiths. They also indicate how culturally developed society must have been to have a demand for this type of object and to appreciate the high level of its workmanship.

Sketch 4: *Gorteenareagh Lock Rings*

Form

The rings are constructed from four main pieces. Two cones are held together with a circular binding strip and a central tube.

Function

They are considered to have been used for holding hair in place. The braided hair could be slipped through the opening into a tube at the centre, and small bosses on the inside were designed to grip it.

Material used

The tubes are made of sheet gold and the surface is made from fine gold wire.

Decorative techniques

The fine wire is closely bound together to form grooves, and this is carefully soldered together without a backing. Soldering, which was the joining of pieces together with molten gold, was a new skill at the time so these objects particularly show how much the skills of craftworkers had advanced. The glittering effect of the fine gold wire bands is, however, also the most decorative element.

(D)

Metalworking

The arrival of metalworking was a key event in Irish history. This new technology had been in Europe from around 4000 BC, but it was to be another 2,000 years before the Neolithic Irish learned these skills. Settlers from France brought the knowledge and art of metallurgy with them, but as the two cultures merged, the native population learned how to mine and process raw ores. Skilled artists and craftsmen soon turned this into finished tools, weapons and ornaments.

Metals

Gold, silver and copper were the first metals worked.

Bronze

Bronze was used for weapons and tools. This is an alloy of copper and tin, and is stronger than pure copper. Copper was found in Ireland but the tin was probably imported from Wales. Mount Gabriel in Cork is one of the few known Bronze Age mines. It dates from 1500–1200 BC, and copper was mined here. Archaeologists believe the walls were heated with fire before being splashed with water to shatter them and extract the metal.

Gold

No ancient gold mines have ever been found, but gold is known to have existed in many parts of the country. **Alluvial gold** was washed down in the rivers and streams in the Wicklow Hills. These small gold particles would be washed with water before being melted and cast into larger pieces.

A huge array of very impressive gold objects from the Bronze Age are on display in the National Museum in Dublin. Most of these were found in the bogs of Ireland and it is possible that others still lie deep in its preserving layers. We will never know who placed these beautiful artefacts there but they tell their own story of a very culturally developed society.

Exam time

Breakdown of marks

- Leaving Certificate Art is marked on a total of 400 marks. The History and Appreciation of Art paper carries 150 marks, so it accounts for 37.5% of your overall grade in Art.
- Answer three questions on the paper.
- Choose one question only from each section, i.e. one question from Section I, one question from Section II and one question from Section III.
- Each question carries 50 marks.
- As a general rule, 40 marks are awarded for the written answer and 10 for sketches.
- If the question is accompanied by a colour illustration, it is likely that 45 marks will be awarded for the written answer and 5 for sketches.

Time management

- The time allowed for the exam is 2½ hours.
- Since each question carries equal marks, it is essential that you divide your time equally between the questions.
- Work out a time plan that allows you enough time for writing and sketching.
- Stick to your time plan, so that you don't end up rushing the last question.
- Use a watch in the exam so that you can keep an eye on the time!

Suggested time plan for the exam paper

- Take **5 minutes** at the start to read the complete section of the paper relevant to your studies. In these 5 minutes, make sure you:
  - Carefully select the questions you are going to answer.
  - Pay special attention to questions with colour illustrations.
  - Look carefully at the two questions in Section II: European Art on art movements or styles and named artworks by a named artist.
  - Read through the questions in Section III: General Appreciation carefully. Some of these are open and general and give plenty of scope for your own interests and ideas.
- Give each question 45 minutes.
- Spend 35 minutes on your written answer and 10 minutes on accompanying sketches.
- Leave 10 minutes at the end of the exam to polish up sketches or tidy up loose ends in your written answers.

Your answers

- Students frequently ask how long each essay should be. As a rough guide, you should write two and a half pages of A4 paper, accompanied by three sketches.

- If you attempt to write or draw more, you are likely to run out of time.

- Write the number of the question in the margin. If the question has part a and b, write this in the margin also.

Make sure the number in the margin corresponds to your answer. **If you change your mind, change the number!** Remember, your answer will be marked according to the number.

- Avoid using memorised set pieces. These may not be relevant and might lead you off the point. Remember: no marks can be given for irrelevant information.

- Write as if your examiner has never heard of anything related to the artwork you are discussing. Never assume that your reader knows what you are talking about.

- Attempt an answer in all three sections: never leave one out! You will pick up at least some marks for an attempt. Remember: losing an entire 50 marks is equal to not turning up for the Life Drawing exam.

- Sketches:
  - Make drawings that clarify your points in a visual way.
  - Label and use tone or colour if appropriate.
  - Add notes to draw attention to particular points.

The question with an illustration is a good choice if you find that sketches take too much time. Marking schemes can vary, but quite often **only 5 marks** are awarded for sketches, so two at most is all you need. It also means, however, that you cannot rely on drawing for extra marks.

SECTION 1

Art in Ireland

Pre-Christian and Early Christian Ireland – Chapters 2 and 3

- Develop a factual knowledge as well as a critical awareness of the artefacts, artistic styles and historical background of your chosen study area
- Explore the wide range of practical techniques used by artists of this time
- Acquire an understanding of how these works of art are related to the function and materials used
- Be aware of outside influences on the development of early Irish art
- Identify the relationships between art and society

Architecture in Eighteenth-Century Georgian Ireland – Chapter 4

- Learning aims on page 77

Stone Age or Megalithic Period (7000–2000 BC)

	Example	Form/Structure	Decoration	Function
Portal tomb/dolmen	Poulnabrone, Co. Clare. Kilclooney, Co. Donegal. Brownshill, Co. Carlow.	Three to seven upright stones carrying one or two very heavy capstones that slope downwards towards the back.		Above-ground burial chambers.
Court cairn	Creevykeel, Co. Sligo.	A semicircular forecourt of upright stones leading to a gallery divided into separate chambers surrounded by an oval-shaped cairn or mound of stones.		Possibly used as burial places or as places of ritual or gathering.
Passage grave	Newgrange, Co. Meath. Dowth, Co. Meath. Knowth, Co. Meath. Located on a bend of the River Boyne.	Layout: Large tombs. Structure: Above-ground cross-shaped passage and chambers covered by a large man-made mound of earth and stones. The mound is surrounded by a circle of kerbstones and large standing stones. Building techniques: Corbel vaulting in the chambers. Large standing stones with cross beam roof stones on the passages.	Location: Entrance wall – white quartz stone. Decoration on the stones on the entrance, passage and roof. Technique: Pocking (carving/incision). Style: A range of abstract, geometric motifs consisting of circles, U-shaped arcs, parallel lines, sun-like shapes, spirals and ovals as well as triangles, zigzags, dots, chevrons and lozenges.	Burial chamber for cremated remains stored in decorated pottery urns. Possible place of worship.

	Example	Form/ Structure	Decoration	Function
The Great Mound	Knowth, Co. Meath.	Layout: Large mound surrounded by many satellite or small tombs. Two passages with separate entrances. The eastern passage is longer and ends in a cruciform shape. Both passages are lined with decoratively carved orthostats (standing stones).	Passages lined with decorated standing stones. Kerbstones decorated with spirals similar to those at Newgrange. Patterns based on diamonds and chevron.	Burial tombs.

Mesolithic Period or Middle Stone Age (7000–3700 BC)

The first human settlers lived by hunting and gathering and settled mostly near riverbanks and lakes.

Neolithic Period or New Stone Age (3700–2000 BC)

- When the Neolithic or New Stone Age farmers arrived, they began clearing the land of trees. This caused the soil to erode and peat bogs formed.
- A great deal of archaeological material was preserved beneath the bogs.
- Pottery, including ornamented cooking pots, was brought by the new settlers of the Neolithic Period.
- Housing became more permanent with dwellings of circular and rectangular shapes.
- Changes to the landscape occurred because of tree-clearing. By the end of the Neolithic Period, communities were spread all over the island.
- There is evidence that people were in regular overseas contact.

Megalithic monuments

Stone burial monuments are evidence of strong spiritual beliefs in Neolithic people.

These include:

- Portal dolmens.
- Court cairns.
- Passage tombs.

key point

Mega = Huge.

Lithos = Large stone.

Megalithic monuments = Great stone monuments.

Orthostat = An upright stone or slab.

key point

Learn by drawing!
Use drawing as a memory aid for each tomb and write notes around it.

Portal dolmens

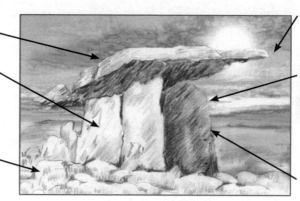

Large limestone capstone

Lower back stone supporting roof stone

The cairn

The tomb lies in the centre of this. The burial chamber was 25 cm deep.

Entrance to the chamber facing north

Portal stones that are 1.8m tall. Stones on either side of the stone chamber support the capstone.

A portico is formed by the three upright limestone stones. The heavier end of the roof stone lies above this.

Example: Poulnabrone Portal Tomb or Dolmen, Co. Clare

The location of this dramatic structure on a low hill suggests it was designed to be seen from a great distance and to be the main visual focus of the surrounding area. During excavations, the remains of 22 adults, children and babies were found in the burial chamber. The bodies were not cremated.

Structure

- This portal tomb or dolmen consists of a large capstone resting on two large upright stones, two more orthostats and an end stone.
- It is surrounded by an oval-shaped cairn or mound of stones that helps to hold it in place.
- The surrounding cairn of stones remains at its original level. This means the structure was never covered and always stood well above ground level.

Court cairns

Cairn or mound of stones

Narrow entrance to the court set into the middle of the cairn

The burial gallery is divided by upright stones into two chambers

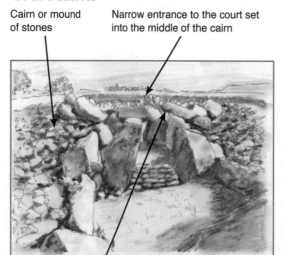

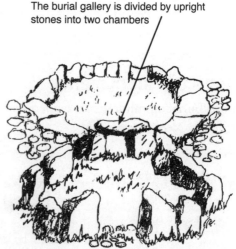

An oval-shaped court lined with upright stones

Example: Creevykeel Court Tomb, Co. Sligo

Located at the foot of the mountains near the sea at Mullaghmore, this is one of the finest examples in Ireland of a full-court tomb. It was excavated in 1935 and shortly afterwards restored. The remains of four cremation burials were found, along with some Neolithic pottery, flint arrow heads, polished stone axes and other artifacts.

Structure

- The tomb consists of a wedge-shaped cairn about 50 m long.
- A narrow entrance lined with upright stones leads to an oval-shaped courtyard and a two-chambered gallery.
- These burial chambers would have originally been covered by a corbelled roof.

Passage tombs

- Newgrange.
- Knowth.
- Dowth.

Learn the appropriate vocabulary relating to the Megalithic Period so that you can comfortably use it in your essays.

Function

- Used as burial places; cremated remains were placed inside.
- May have been a place for ceremonies.
- Offered a focal point for communities.

Ornamented stones

- Abstract and geometric repeating patterns of circles and whirls.
- Patterns are likely to have an astronomical connection or relate to a form of calendar.
- Patterns may have had religious meaning.

See more at www. voicesfromthedawn.com/ newgrange

Newgrange, Co. Meath

The passage grave at Newgrange, Co. Meath, dates back to approximately 3000 BC.

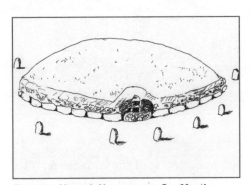

Passage Mound, Newgrange, Co. Meath

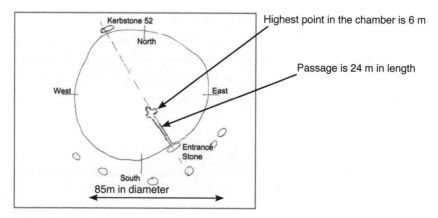

Plan and dimensions

Form

- A large mound or cairn of stones is cut through with a long passage. Inside there are three chambers.
- The mound is surrounded by a kerb of massive slabs and encircled by 12 tall monoliths or standing stones.

The winter solstice

- At sunrise on 21 December (the winter solstice) the light shines through a special roof box above the entrance.
- The light runs along the passage and the floor of the chamber. It is lit up for 17 minutes.

Corbelled roof

The roof of the chamber is corbelled: slabs are placed on top of each other so that each one partly overlaps the one beneath as they gradually rise in height.

Entrance stone

The entrance stone is the most spectacular of the kerbstones. It has carvings of a triple spiral, double spirals, concentric semicircles and lozenges.

Kerbstones

- There are 97 huge kerbstones surrounding the great mound.
- Kerbstone 52 is at the back of the mound and lines up directly with the entrance stone. The entrance stone and kerbstone 52 share many similar markings.

Basin stones

- Large stones with a sunken centre are found in the chambers at Newgrange. These are called basin stones.
- It is likely that the basin stones were used to hold bones or the cremated remains of the dead.

key point

Tip for sketching the entrance stone at Newgrange: Draw the line in the centre. Next, draw the three spirals on the left and four on the right. Then fill in the lozenges.

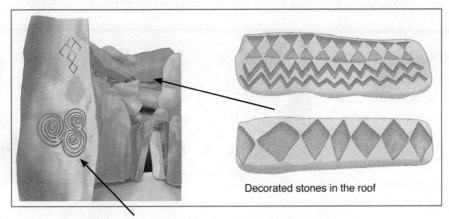

Decorated stones in the roof

A decorated orthostat in the passage showing a three-spiral pattern

Corbelled roof in the chamber

A large capstone rests on the centre. The outer edges of the corbels are sloped downwards to keep the interior dry.

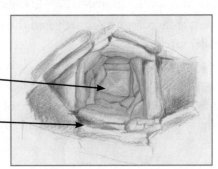

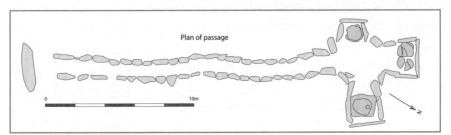

Plan of passage

0   10m

Plan of the long passage showing the cruciform shape of the chambers at the end. It is lined on both sides with large upright stones or 'orthostats'.

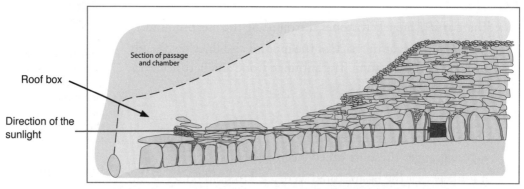

Section of the tomb at Newgrange showing the light shining directly through the roof box, allowing a narrower stream to project deep into the chamber

Kerbstone 52

This is situated at the back of the mound in direct line with the entrance stone. The two stones have many similar markings.

Knowth

- Knowth is similar in size to Newgrange.
- Recent archaeology has uncovered the mound and 18 smaller satellite mounds.
- The art is really special at Knowth. It is believed that a quarter of Europe's Neolithic art is held here.
- Knowth remained a significant place of political and military power right up to Christian times.

Form

- A great mound with two passages opposite each other.
- The passages have separate entrances that do not connect.
- The eastern passage is longer and ends in a cruciform shape.
- Both passages are lined with decoratively carved orthostats.

key point

In terms of archaeology, art, beauty and size, Knowth is far more impressive than Newgrange.

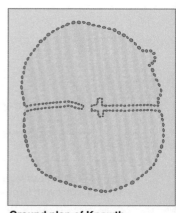

Ground plan of Knowth

Basin stone

- In a recess at the end of the eastern passage is a richly decorated granite basin stone.
- The basin stone is decorated with parallel horizontal scoring on the outside and with arcs and rays on the inside.
- Behind the basin stone is a large orthostat engraved with symbols.

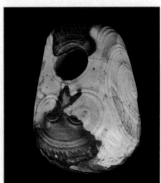

Engraved kerbstone at Knowth. Kerbstone 15 is possibly a sundial or lunar calendar.

Kerbstones

- There are 127 oblong kerbstones surrounding the great mound.
- The slabs were probably transported from several miles away.
- Angular and spiral inscriptions stop at ground level. This suggests that the stones were already in place before the art was applied.
- This impressive art suggests that the people were highly aware of astronomical function.
- Several kerbstones display symbolism that may be linked to the lunar calendar.

Mace-head

- A decorative flint mace-head was found during archaeological excavations.
- It is carved in low-relief style.
- The hole was probably for a wooden handle.

Knowth Mace-head, National Museum of Ireland

Dowth

- Dowth was built in the same period as Newgrange and Knowth and is similar to them in size.
- Considerable damage was done to Dowth when it was excavated in an unprofessional manner in 1847.

Questions on the Stone Age can vary significantly. The Ordinary Level question focuses on information and facts relating to Newgrange, but the Higher Level question asks you to discuss a statement and to focus on particular aspects of the Mesolithic and Neolithic Periods

2015 Ordinary Level paper: Section I, Question 1

The site illustrated on the accompanying sheet is from the Neolithic Period. Answer (a), (b) and (c).

(a) Name the site.

(b) Describe and discuss the site under the following headings:

- Location
- Structure
- Function

(c) Sketch, describe and discuss the decoration on one of this site's main features. *Illustrate your answer.*

Marking scheme

Q.		Marks	Notes
A	Name of the site	5	
B	Description and discussion of site under headings: location, function, structure	25	Location – 5 Function – 5 Structure – 15
C	Description and discussion of decoration on one of the site's main features	15	5 for name 10 for discussion
D	Sketches	5	
	Total	50	

2017 Higher Level paper: Section I, Question 1

'There are many documented Stone Age tombs in Ireland that reveal a wealth of information about the lives of the people who built them.'

Discuss this statement with reference to two named stone tombs that you have studied. In your answer refer to the structure, function and location of each of the examples you have chosen.

and

Briefly describe and discuss the motifs and stone working techniques used to decorate Stone Age tombs.

Illustrate your answer.

SAMPLE EXAM QUESTION

Questions may also focus on a certain aspect of the art in question. Note the following example of a question that requires you to concentrate only on carved decoration:

'The passage tombs in the Boyne valley show a high level of technical sophistication in carved decoration.'

Discuss this statement with reference to two examples of decorated stones. In your answer refer also to the location, motifs and the techniques used in the execution of this decoration.

and

Briefly discuss what we know of the people who carved these stones and their beliefs.

Marking scheme

Q.		Marks	Notes
A	Discussion of statement with reference to named decorated stones, discussing and describing the location, motifs and techniques	20	5 for named carved stones and 15 for discussion
B	Description and discussion of two named decorated stones	15	3 for 1st named stone and 5 for discussion 2 for 2nd named stone and 5 for discussion
C	Brief discussion on the people who carved these stones and their spiritual beliefs	5	
D	Sketches	10	
	Total	50	

SAMPLE ANSWER

The carved decoration on so many stones from the Neolithic Period in the Boyne Valley region is highly impressive and shows that people of that time had reached a very high level of technical skill. The sophistication of the designs also gives us a real insight into the possible spiritual beliefs of people living at that time in pre-Christian Ireland. These complex patterns were carved over 3,000 years ago and they show us how incredibly advanced these Neolithic people were, especially considering they did not have the advantage of the technology we have today.

Location

Some of the most amazing Neolithic stone carvings can be found at Knowth, Dowth and Newgrange. These three passage tombs, situated near each other in a bend on the river Boyne in Co. Meath, are made entirely from massive stones.

Sitting on a hill overlooking the river Newgrange is the most famous of the tombs. This highly impressive structure is made up of a loose circular cairn of stone that covers a tomb and is surrounded by a 'Great Circle' of tall, wide orthostats that were erected after its construction. There were originally 35 stones in this circle, but only 12 remain today.

A kerb of massive slabs surround the base of the cairn and act as a retaining wall. These are laid on their long edges with their ends touching, and some are placed in sockets to maintain the continuous circle. There are 97

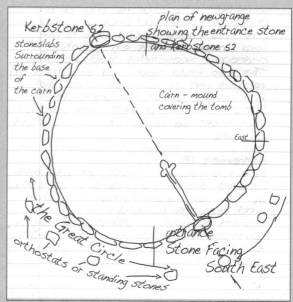

Plan of Newgrange

of these stones in total but only 29 are exposed. Two of these in particular display some jaw-dropping and highly skilled decoration. These are the entrance stone, which is located to the front, and Kerbstone 52 which lines up directly with this at the back.

The entrance stone

The most famous of all the stones at Newgrange lies directly in front of the entrance. The carved decoration on this shows a particularly high level of technical sophistication. It has curvilinear markings of triple spirals, double spirals, concentric semicircles and lozenges, with a vertical line separating the circles. On the right-hand side of the stone are two double spirals that sit on wavy lines, and on the left is a triple spiral with a series of lozenge shapes. This line or groove between these sets of patterns lines up directly with the centre of the entrance space behind it and the lintel above, which suggests it may have had a calendrical or religious meaning, or perhaps it was used in rituals or community gatherings.

Kerbstone 52

Kerbstone 52 lies at the back of the mound and has very similar markings of spirals, concentric semicircles and lozenges to the entrance stone, but is also more

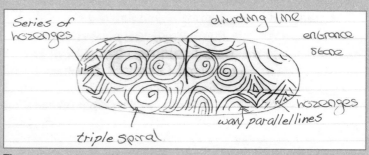

The entrance stone at Newgrange

varied, and, if anything, is even more impressive. It too is has a groove down the centre but the left side is also divided across. The upper half is covered by a double spiral and two

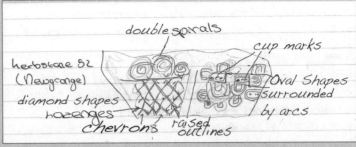

Kerbstone 52

smaller spirals with lozenges or diamond shapes carved into the surface below to leave raised crisscrossed outlines. A series of chevrons runs along the end of this. The left-hand side has a series of ovals with cup marks in the centres that are connected by arcs.

Decoration and motifs

These settlers created artistic designs that were miles ahead in their artistic sophistication when compared to others from this age. The abstract, non-representational, geometric designs included motifs such as circles, dots, spirals, arcs and radials, with spoke-like lines fanning out from the centre, as well as parallel lines, zigzags, chevrons, lozenges and many more that were all drawn free-hand. Cup shapes, concentric circles and the famous tri-circles are found within and outside the tomb at Newgrange. No natural representations of humans or

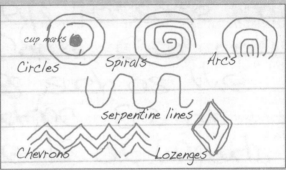

Decorations and motifs on the Newgrange stones

animals are visible, but it is associated with some truly unique designs. The carvers seem to have very carefully marked out the designs to pick up the sunlight. This is true especially of the entrance stone and on the lintel above it.

Techniques

The people who built Newgrange and the other tombs in the Boyne Valley must have used a log-and-pulley system to move such heavy weights. Some of the stone even came from different counties and would have had to have been moved by boat, e.g. quartz came from Co. Wicklow and granite came from Co. Louth. Most of the stones at these passage tombs have been dressed (cut into shape) and the people had to make their own tools in order to carve all the different patterns and textures. They were made by chip carving, which includes banging shapes in the stone with sharp flint or another hard stone tool to create designs and motifs. Tools such as axels and chisels were used in these designs and the skill of pocking can also be seen on the stones. The technique of pecking or picking was the cutting out of lines and dots with a sharp chisel or point driven by a hammer. Designs were incised, which left other parts of the stone surface in raised relief.

The Neolithic people and their spiritual beliefs

The carvings show that the builders had great artistic sensibility and it definitely must have carried some meaning for the Neolithic builders of Newgrange. They could have religious meaning, which tells us they most likely believed in the afterlife. For example, the triple circle design on a standing stone inside the tomb must have had some significance beyond the aesthetic. It could have represented some aspect of the afterlife or it could have represented the sun, but in the end we can only guess the true meaning of these decorated textures.

We do know, however, that Newgrange was a burial ground, and that it may have had other functions such as an assembly place for the settled people. Ceremonies for worshipping the dead could have taken place there. The builders must have believed in the supernatural, since they built a sacred place for their dead. They left possessions with their dead, which suggests that they believed in an afterlife.

The designs may have also had some kind of calendrical meaning, possibly related to the different seasons. It is very likely that the people were highly aware of astronomical function because each year, on 21 December (the winter solstice), the sun shines through a roof box which faces south-east just above the lintel over the entrance and lights up the passage for a few minutes as it rises at dawn. This tells us that the builders had a great understanding of the movement of the sun.

This close connection with the winter solstice probably means that Newgrange was a site of celebration for a new year of farming or for sun worship, but we will never be sure. What is certain though is that builders of the tombs in Boyne Valley were intelligent, superstitious and incredibly skilled in many ways. They possessed engineering, architectural and organisational skills that enabled them to build these enormous structures. They were also artistic and creative and their sophisticated decorations are just as impressive today as no doubt they were in ancient times.

R. O'Driscoll, 2017

Bronze Age Ireland (2000–500 BC)

New settlers arrived in Ireland from France about 2000 BC and brought the skills of metalworking, especially in bronze.

Great changes came about as a result because:

- Bronze was a far stronger material than stone.
- It could be moulded into a required shape.
- Metal axes made tree-cutting easier.

The Beaker People

Some settlers also brought the skill of pottery-making. They became known as the 'Beaker People' because their cremation burials were placed under upturned 'beaker'-shaped pots. These pots were very highly decorated.

Beaker Pottery: Early Bronze Age (2500–1500 BC)				
Artefact	Examples	Form	Decoration	Function
Food vessels Burial urns Earthenware bowls Vases 	Bowl-shaped food vessel (Aghnahily, Co. Laois). Vase-shaped food vessel (Topped Mountain, Co. Fermanagh). Vase urn (Priestdown, Co. Down). Encrusted urn (Newtown, Co. Limerick).	Small, squat, rounded bowls or taller V-shaped, narrow-based vases 10 cm to 20 cm high.	Incised patterns made with a comb. Slanted lines in a herringbone motif and cross-hatched triangles. Encrusted or applied relief strip lattice ornament.	Funerary vessels for cremated ashes or to accompany the dead in tombs.

Everyday life in Bronze Age Ireland

Agriculture

- The growth in population created pressure to find farmland, so large areas of forests were cleared.
- This caused the land to become wetter, and a thick blanket of peat bog developed.

Houses

- Only a very small amount of evidence for housing exists.
- This suggests that rectangular or circular houses were made from wooden beams and had wattle-and-daub walls with thatched roofs.
- These would have been similar to Neolithic dwellings.

Beliefs and burials

- Burials often took place in small rectangular tombs called cists. Bodies were placed in a crouched position and covered over with stone and earth.
- Tools, weapons and a small, bowl-shaped piece of pottery were often put with the body.
- Stone circles, stone rows, and standing stones all date from the Bronze Age.
- Large numbers of gold ornaments have been found in the bogs of Ireland, and may have been placed there as 'offerings'.
- All of this indicates that there may have been a belief in an afterlife.

Cooking

- Communal cooking may have taken place at a 'fulacht fiadh'. These were wood-lined troughs in the ground, filled with water.
- A fire was used to heat stones, which were then thrown into the water to bring it to boil and cook the meat.
- Large cauldrons were also used for cooking (see page 44).

Metalwork

Settlers brought the art of metallurgy from France to Ireland. The Neolithic people soon learned how to mine and process raw ores, and craftsmen turned them into finished pieces. Gold, silver and copper were the first metals worked.

Copper

The earlier part of the Bronze Age is sometimes referred to as the Copper Age. Copper was used in a pure state.

Bronze

Bronze is an alloy of copper and tin. Copper was found in Ireland, but it is likely that tin was imported from Wales. Bronze was stronger than pure copper and led to more sophisticated weapons and tools.

Bronze Age mines

- A Bronze Age mine was found at Mount Gabriel, Co. Cork.
- Copper was mined here.
- It dates from 1500–1200 BC and has 25 mine shafts.

> **Mount Gabriel** is one of the few known Bronze Age mines. Archaeologists believe the walls were heated with fire and then splashed with water to shatter them. This made the process of extracting the metal ore easier.

Silver

Silver was mined in the Silvermine Mountains, Co. Tipperary.

Gold

No gold mines have ever been found. It is assumed that **alluvial** gold was found in rivers and streams in the Wicklow Hills.

Gold ornaments

Gold was first used in Bronze Age Ireland. It was worked in much the same way as bronze, but because gold is such a soft metal it had no practical purpose. It is, however, highly desirable for jewellery and ornaments, and these seem to have been in great demand with the society of that time. This suggests there were people of high status and may mean that an 'aristocracy' or royalty had developed.

The word **alluvial** refers to anything that is deposited by flowing water, e.g. silt, sand, clay or gravel. Gold nuggets or dust found in this state are called alluvial gold.

The National Museum of Ireland in Dublin has one of the largest and finest collections of Bronze Age gold ornaments in the world. Many spectacular pieces of gold jewellery have been found over the years, particularly in boglands.

The Bronze Age has three distinct periods:

- Early (2000–1500 BC).
- Middle (1500–1200 BC).
- Late (1200–500 BC).

Early Bronze Age (2000–1500 BC)

Gold-working techniques

Gold was beaten into a thin sheet using a hammer. This was then cut into the required shape and decorated.

Decoration

Patterns were abstract and geometric. Compasses were used for circular decoration.

Decorative techniques included:

- **Repoussé:** Hammering a design on the back of the thin sheet of gold.
- **Incision:** Cutting a design into the front.

Learn by making!
Cut out the objects in light card. Make incised decoration using a pointed instrument. Repoussé using a ballpoint pen on the reverse. Colour them in gold and paste them into your sketchbook.

Metalwork: Early Bronze Age (2500–1500 BC)					
Artefact	Examples	Form	Decoration	Function	Metalwork Technique
Discs	Pair of gold 'sun discs' (Tedavnet, Co. Monaghan).	Small discs of thin sheet gold 11.6 cm in diameter. Often found in pairs.	Cross motif of chevrons and zigzags. Repoussé technique.	Small holes near the centre suggest stitching to garments – possibly worn on the chest.	Circle cut from a thin beaten plate of gold. Decorated by hammering and punching.
Lunulae	Gold lunula (Ross, Co. Westmeath).	Crescent or half-moon shapes. 20 cm across.	Combinations of lines, zigzags and hatched triangles. Incision (cutting) technique.	Likely to have been worn as neck ornaments.	Shape cut from thin beaten sheets of gold with slightly thicker extensions at the ends for locking.

Function

Small holes near the centre suggest it may have been a kind of button. It may have been sewn onto a garment.

Metalwork technique

Gold was beaten into thin sheets with a hammer and cut into discs

Decoration

Repoussé in the form of a cross encircled by concentric bands of chevrons (zigzags)

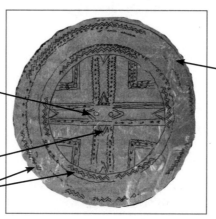

Gold Sun Disc from Tedavnet, Co. Monaghan

Both of these may have been used for ceremonial purposes and worn by someone of high status

Bands of decoration at the pointed ends

Metalwork technique

Gold was beaten into a thin sheet using a hammer and then cut into the crescent shape

Decoration

The decoration is incised (cut on the front). There are bands of decoration with lines and motifs of triangles and chevron strokes.

Paddle-shaped ends are slightly thicker to form a clasp

Designs can be seen clearly on the thin gold sheet coming through on the back

Parallel lines around the edges

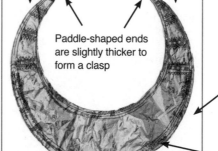

Gold Lunula, Ross, Co. Westmeath

Middle Bronze Age (1500–1200 BC)

The period from 1200 BC onwards was a very prolific time for gold ornaments.

Gold-working techniques

- **Twisting:** Straps of gold were hammered to make narrow bands, then twisted to make neck ornaments, earrings or girdles.
- **Flange twisting:** Thicker bars were hammered at the edges and twisted to make neck ornaments called torcs.

Metalwork: Middle Bronze Age (1500–1200 BC)					
Artefact	Examples	Form	Decoration	Function	Metalwork Technique
Earrings	Flanged gold earrings (Castlerea, Co. Roscommon).	Small, twisted rings with a 'collar' and rod-like ends. 3.6 cm in diameter.	Flanged and twisted.	Worn in the ears.	Four flanges created by hammering out the edges of an angled bar of gold. Twisted to 180°.

Metalwork: Middle Bronze Age (1200–500 BC) Bishopsland Phase (1200–1000 BC, dated to the time of a hoard found in Bishopsland, Co. Kildare) (Sometimes referred to as the Late Bronze Age)					
Artefact	Examples	Form	Decoration	Function	Metalwork Technique
Twisted bands for waist, arm and neck	Gold Ribbon Torc (Belfast, Co. Antrim).	Gold twisted band with locking device. 17.5 cm in diameter.	Twisting.	Worn as a neck ornament.	Strap of gold beaten out from the centre to very thin edges before twisting. Thicker metal forms buttons at the end to interlock.
Bracelets	Gold armlets (Derrinboy, Co. Offaly).	Curved broad bands of gold.	Broad ridges with smaller ridges. Repoussé technique.	Worn as arm bands or bracelets.	Made from a length of broad gold ribbon. Thin edges of the ribbon coiled backwards and inwards to create a strong edge.

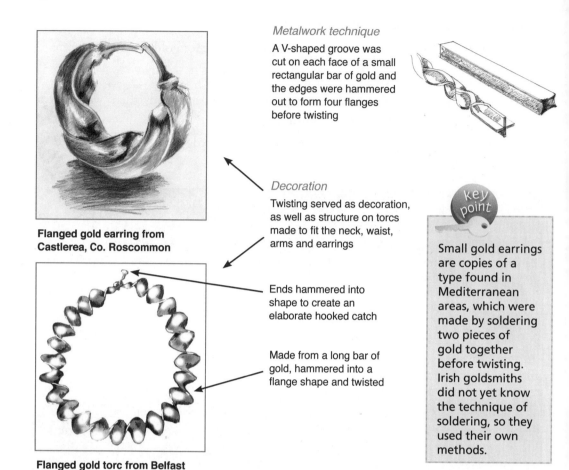

Flanged gold earring from Castlerea, Co. Roscommon

Metalwork technique

A V-shaped groove was cut on each face of a small rectangular bar of gold and the edges were hammered out to form four flanges before twisting

Decoration

Twisting served as decoration, as well as structure on torcs made to fit the neck, waist, arms and earrings

Ends hammered into shape to create an elaborate hooked catch

Made from a long bar of gold, hammered into a flange shape and twisted

Flanged gold torc from Belfast

key point

Small gold earrings are copies of a type found in Mediterranean areas, which were made by soldering two pieces of gold together before twisting. Irish goldsmiths did not yet know the technique of soldering, so they used their own methods.

Late Bronze Age (1200–500 BC)

The late Bronze Age is famous for its huge quantity, quality and variety of gold ornaments. Craftsmanship had reached a very high level of sophistication and is the highest standard known in Europe at the time. This is why the Late Bronze Age is often called Ireland's first Golden Age.

Gold-working techniques

- Repoussé.
- Incision.
- Twisting.
- Gold wire: Very thin strips were twisted to make fine wire. This was used for holding objects together and for decorative purposes.

Metalwork: Late Bronze Age to Golden Age (1200–500 BC) Dowris Phase (900–500 BC, dated to the time of a hoard found in Dowris, Co. Offaly)					
Artefact	Examples	Form	Decoration	Function	Metalwork Technique
Dress fasteners	Gold dress fastener or fibula (Clones, Co. Monaghan)	Large, bow-shaped bar linking two concave bases or terminals. 21.5 cm long.	Engraved concentric circles on the terminals. Parallel bands and chevrons on the bases of the bow.	Garment fastener or double button (probably ceremonial).	Pure gold weighing over 1,000 g. Concave terminals beaten to shape.
Gorgets	Gold gorget (Glenisheen, Co. Clare).	Curved sheet of gold with disc terminals. 31.4 cm in diameter.	Repoussé ridges with recessed rope moulding. Engraved concentric circles enclose a small conical boss on the terminal discs.	Neck ornament.	Semicircular band of beaten sheet gold with rolled edges. Terminal discs linked together by folded edges. A slit in the lower disc allows the band to slip through. Terminals stitched on with gold wire.
Lock rings	Gold hair lock rings (Gorteenreagh, Co. Clare).	Conical shapes with a slit at the side. 10 cm in diameter.	Concentric lines of tiny gold wires placed beside each other.	Likely to have been hair ornaments.	Made from four main pieces: a central split tube, two gapped conical plates and a circular binding strip.
Bulla	Gold-plated bulla (Bog of Allen, Co. Kildare).	Pendant-shaped 'bulla'. 6.4 cm long.	Concentric circles, semicircles, triangles and other patterns in repoussé.	Possibly worn around the neck as a pendant. May have served as an amulet or an object to ward off evil or ensure fertility.	Lead covered with sheet gold.

Form

A connecting bow joins two hollow, cone-shaped terminals

Decorated at the base of the bow with small hatched triangles

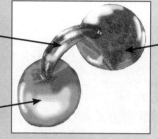

Decoration

Both terminals are decorated with a series of small concentric circles surrounding a central dot

Function

Dress fasteners are like double buttons that fitted into buttonholes. It is likely they were worn for ceremonial purposes.

Gold dress fastener or fibula from Clones, Co. Monaghan

Sleeve fasteners

Sleeve fasteners were similar in design to dress fasteners, but were smaller in size.

Form

A crescent-shaped sheet of gold with a gold disc at each end

Function

Possibly worn hanging from the neck as a chest ornament. Probably a high status object for ceremonial purposes.

Metalwork technique

The shape is cut from gold that is hammered into a very thin sheet

Terminal discs – two circular plates, cover each other to enclose the ends of the collar

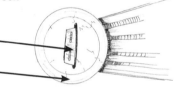

Decorated with concentric circles and repoussé-raised bosses

A narrow strip of gold rolled and pressed around the raw edge

Decorated all over with raised ridges and rope moulding in repoussé

Gleninsheen Gorget, found in a rock crevice in the Burren, Co. Clare

To attach the collar, the edge is inserted into a slit on the under disc and is sewn in place with gold wire

The smaller of the discs is placed on top and the edges of the disc underneath are rolled over to finish the raw edges

Metalwork technique

The grooves on the surface of the cone are made with wires closely bound and finely soldered together

Form

Two cones are held together with a circular binding strip

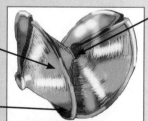

A tubular cone runs through the centre. Small bosses inside this tube were probably for gripping the hair.

Function

Considered to be for holding hair in place

Gold Lock Rings from Gorteenreagh, Co. Clare

Form

A small locket

Decoration

Lead covered in gold foil and decorated with repoussé designs of concentric circles, semicircles, triangles and other patterns. These patterns may form a human face.

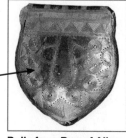

Function

May have been an amulet: a charm worn to ward off evil or to promote fertility. Probably worn about the neck on a chain, like a locket.

Bulla from Bog of Allen, Co. Kildare

Tools and weapons

Artefact	Examples	Form	Decoration	Function	Metalwork Technique
Leather, wood and bronze shields	Bronze shield (Lough Gur, Co. Limerick).	Sheet bronze disc, 72 cm in diameter. A strap of bronze curved to form a handgrip is riveted to the back, 71.3 cm in diameter.	Ridges and rounded bosses. Large raised central boss. Repoussé technique.	Shield for use in combat against a slashing sword. Shields of wood and leather were more common in Ireland. Bronze is very rare.	Bronze thick enough to withstand a sword stroke would be too heavy, so to deflect the blow of the sword, six equally spaced concentric ridges were raised from the surface of a thin plate with six rings of raised bosses between.
Bronze cauldrons	Bronze cauldron (Castlederg, Co. Tyrone).	Sheet bronze cooking pot with turned-out rim and handles, 56 cm in diameter.	Pointed rivets that hold the plates of sheet bronze together may also have collected heat to speed up the boiling process.	Cooking vessel for meat with two large rings to suspend it from a pole and carry it to a feast.	The rim is formed from the in-turned edge of the disc. Base formed by a dished bronze circular plate. Above this are three rounds of sheet bronze plates riveted together. Two pieces form the upper round. Handles are securely fastened to the rim with straps of bronze.

Form
A strap of bronze riveted to the back of the shield is curved to form a handgrip

Metalwork technique
Blows directed at the shield would have bounced off the ridges and rounded boxes, and reduced the force

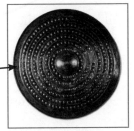

Function
Probably for decorative purposes only, because it is too thin to be really effective

Bronze ceremonial shield from Lough Gur, Co. Limerick

Function

Large cauldrons were used for cooking meat. Large rings allow it to be suspended from a pole and carried to a fiest.

Metalwork technique

Two heavy fittings, which hold the lifting handles, are securely attached to the rim

Metal sheets were fastened together by high-pointed rivets. This is an excellent example of the technical brilliance achieved in sheet-bronze work.

Bronze cauldron, from Castlederg, Co. Tyrone

Iron Age and La Tène (1200 BC–AD 15)

Metalwork: 500 BC–AD 100					
Artefact	Examples	Form	Decoration	Function	Metalwork Technique
Torcs, collars and neck rings	Gold torc, 19.4 cm in diameter, found at Broighter, Co. Derry in a hoard of gold ornaments. This included a model of a boat with tiny oars.	Two conjoined half hoops with a decorative fastener.	Two interlocking curves of repoussé foliage trumpets and spiral bosses. Plain surfaces covered in compass-incised fine lines.	Neck ornament.	Decorated flat, gold plates rolled around a form and soldered. Tubes then filled with hot resin and bent into hoops.

The end of the Bronze Age

The Irish Bronze Age is generally accepted to have died away around 500 BC when people from Europe associated with the superior Iron Age culture arrived in Ireland. These people are more popularly known as the Celts. They arrived in Britain and Ireland around 500 BC and within a few hundred years Celtic culture had taken over across the entire island.

Art as evidence

- The Celts had not discovered writing, so they left no firsthand documentary sources.
- The main evidence of the influence of the Celts in Ireland is found in Celtic-style artwork.
- Objects with Celtic-style decoration were found mostly in the north and north-western parts of the country.

The word **Celts** comes from 'Keltoi', a term used by the Ancient Greeks to describe a large community or tribe of central Europeans. There are two distinct groups of Celts:

- **Hallstatt Celts** (1200–475 BC).
- **La Tène Celts** (500 BC to the first century AD).

Hallstatt Celts (1200–475 BC)

The Hallstatt Celts lived in the area around Hallstatt in central Austria. They became wealthy and influential through their control of the following crucial trade goods:

- **Copper** and **tin**, which were important for bronze.
- **Salt**, which was crucial for preservation of food.
- **Iron**, which gave them strong technological advantages.

Artefact	Examples	Form	Decoration	Function	Metalwork Technique
Trumpets, discs, swords and scabbards	Bronze trumpet from Lougnashade, Co. Armagh, 186.5 cm long.	Very long tubular curved trumpet with a rimmed circular bronze disc at the mouth.	Disc decorated with curvilinear spirals, wiry curves, tendrils and bosses in high relief. Repoussé technique.	Musical instrument.	Tube made by rolling edges of a sheet of bronze and riveting them to an interior strip.
Bronze crown	Petrie Crown (named after antiquarian George Petrie), 15 cm high.	Fragment. Circular discs mounted on a band of bronze. Conical horns rise from behind discs.	Curvilinear low-relief patterns produced by cutting away the metal. Enamel bosses on the discs. Oval curves and ornamental birdheads on the horns.	Possibly a crown. Small perforations on the hoops suggest stitching to fabric.	The base is riveted to the band, which is brazed to the discs. A folded sheet of bronze forms the shape of the horns with the edges riveted to an under sheet of copper.

Iron

Iron was a far superior metal because it was stronger and more durable than bronze. It required much hotter fires to extract it from its ore, so working with iron required considerable skill. Iron became very popular, but bronze also continued to be used.

Wealth

Richly adorned tombs, assumed to be those of chieftains or royalty, were found in places associated with major Hallstatt cultural centres.

Art

- The Hallstatt style brought together several artistic traditions of European art styles.
- It was influenced by Greek and Italian art.
- Rigid geometric forms were most common.

La Tène Celts (500–15 BC)

- La Tène culture is named after the site near Lake Neuchâtel in Switzerland.
- La Tène people spread rapidly throughout Europe and occupied the lands that are now Switzerland, Belgium, Germany, the Netherlands, Brittany and Britain, before bringing their culture to Ireland.

Ceremonial offerings

- La Tène is one of the most important Celtic sites. It is believed that part of the culture involved throwing objects into lakes as a ceremonial offering.
- A huge quantity of exceptionally fine weapons and other objects were found in the lake at La Tène.

Irish La Tène art

Influences

- La Tène culture had contacts far and wide throughout Europe.
- It was mainly influenced by Eastern and Greek foliage sources from the Mediterranean.
- It developed unique abstract compositions.

> **key point**
>
> La Tène developed unique abstract compositions of curvilinear patterns that flow over surfaces in themes of great vigour and originality.

Motifs and patterns

- Motifs in La Tène art are based on plant forms, e.g. honeysuckle and palm leaves with flowing leafy tendrils.
- Curvilinear patterns include waves, spirals and s-scrolls.
- An offshoot of the Waldalgesheim style reached Ireland. This style takes its name from a chieftain's grave near Bonn in Germany, where some highly ornate objects have been found.

Art as evidence of the Celts in Ireland

- Beautifully decorated metalwork found by archaeologists shows the spread of the La Tène culture in Europe from about 400 BC.
- Irish La Tène is unique in its style and it continued to develop long after European examples had become obsolete.

Metalwork technique

The Celts brought skills such as soldering and enamelling and this was incorporated into Irish workmanship.

Metals used during the La Tène Period in Ireland

- Iron was used for implements and weapons.
- Bronze continued to be used for practical as well as ornamental objects.
- Gold was used for ornamental objects.

Iron objects

Very few items made of iron have survived. However, some very fine swords and scabbards have been found in various places in Ireland, mainly in Co. Antrim.

Bronze objects

A fine example of a bronze object from this period is the Loughnashade Trumpet from the first century BC.

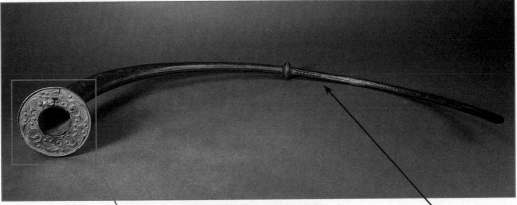

The Loughnashade Trumpet, Co. Armagh

A long, large, curved stem

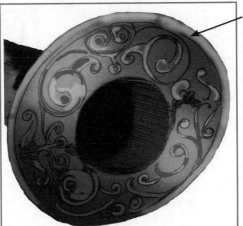

Form

Two curved tubes of bronze with a joint in the middle form an elongated conical shape that opens to the trumpet mouth

Metalwork technique

A sheet of bronze was rolled to make the tube. This was riveted to a strip of metal on the inside.

Decoration

The rimmed circular disc at the trumpet mouth is decorated with high-relief repoussé curvilinear designs

Function

This Celtic trumpet was probably used as an instrument of war. It is likely that it was s-shaped and played with the two parts bending in opposite directions.

Form

Circular, concave-
shaped discs are
mounted on a band
of metal with conical
horns behind

The two discs have
individual patterns

A stud of red enamel
in the central boss

Decorated in low-relief curvilinear patterns, cut away rather than
repoussé. The design continues over the rivets, indicating that it
was cut away after the horn was in position.

Metalwork technique

The horns were made by folding
a sheet of bronze into a conical
shape and riveting the edges to
an under sheet of copper

Stylised bird heads

The original function is unknown
but a row of small holes on the
band suggests that fabric may
have been stitched to it

The Petrie Crown

Gold objects

The Broighter Hoard

A hoard found at Broighter, Co. Derry is the richest collection of gold objects from Iron
Age Ireland. Unfortunately, when the hoard was discovered by farmers ploughing a
field, some damage was caused to the items. The hoard consisted of:

- A little boat with oars and a mast.
- A bowl.
- Two chain necklaces.

- Two twisted necklaces.
- A collar (torc).

This neck ornament probably
originally had a hinge for
opening (this was missing
when it was found)

Raised spiral bosses – clipped
on to give the appearance of
flower heads

**The
Broighter
Collar**

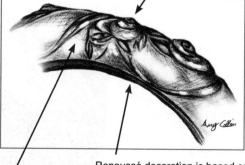

A torc is made in two half hoops with
an elaborate locking device attached
to the front end of each

Plain spaces at both sides
decorated with fine compass-
drawn lines

Repoussé decoration is based on
foliage and leaf motifs. Combines
older, traditional methods of
decoration with the newer, more
decorative La Tène style.

Metalworking technique

Decorated sheets of gold were rolled into tubes and soldered together.
These were then filled with hot wax to heat the metal before bending into
hoops. The decoration was applied to the sheets of gold while they were
flat.

Decorated stones			
Artefact	Form	Decoration	Function
Turoe Stone, Co. Galway	Domed granite boulder. Cut to shape. Approximately 1.68 m high.	Incised decoration. Step-like pattern around the middle. Upper body covered with curvilinear ornament of trumpet ends, triskeles and stylised animal heads.	Probably for use in ritual.
Castlestrange Stone, Co. Roscommon	Rounded boulder.	Swirls and spirals carved into the stone.	Probably for use in ritual.

Decorated stones

A large number of carved stones were created in the late Iron Age in Ireland. It is not known what purpose they served, but it was probably for some kind of ritual. The complex, swirling patterns on these are similar to those found on central European Celtic culture ornaments.

Examples

- The Turoe Stone, Co. Galway.
- The Castlestrange Stone, Co. Roscommon.

The Turoe Stone

- The stone was moved to its present location on the lawn in front of Turoe House, Co. Galway in the mid-nineteenth century. Before that, it stood for centuries at a *lios* (fairy fort) some distance away.
- Its size and weight and the fact it is carved from local stone suggest that it was carved on the spot.
- The function of this large, rounded stone pillar is unknown. The surface is smoothed and covered completely with decoration.

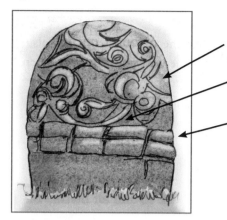

The Turoe Stone

Decoration

The background is carefully chiselled away to produce the low-relief decoration

Leafy curvilinear designs – spirals, circles and curves in undulating whirls

A band of geometric patterns similar to a Greek steppattern encircling the base

A single triskele (a three-legged motif of trumpet curves) appears in the centre of one of the panels

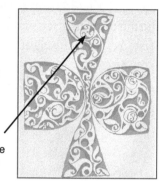

Expanded drawing of the ornament on the Turoe Stone, showing that while the pattern is all over the stone, it is planned to have four distinct sides

Castlestrange Stone

The Castlestrange Stone is located at Castlestrange House, near Athleague, Co. Roscommon.

Decoration

- A continuous swirling pattern.
- This is engraved, rather than carved in relief like the Turoe Stone.

Ogham stones

- Irish was written for the first time using the Ogham script made up of groups of strokes set in lines or angles.
- Pillar stones or boulders displaying Ogham are found mostly along the south coast of Ireland.

Figures and heads

- Some representations of Celtic gods have been found in Ireland.
- These are mostly made of stone, although wooden examples have also been found.
- Stone heads with a number of faces were found throughout the Celtic world.

Examples in Ireland

- A finely carved head with three faces, in Corleck, Co. Cavan.
- Stone figure, Tandragee, Co. Armagh.
- Figures on Boa Island, Co. Fermanagh. The date of these figures is uncertain, but it is possible that they date back to the Iron Age.

Stone figure, Tandragee, Co. Armagh

The influence of Celtic art

The influence of Celtic art lasted far longer in Ireland than the rest of Europe. Spirals, curvilinear motifs and other Celtic decoration were continued by artists and craftsmen during the Christian era. Celtic motifs can be found on some of the great treasures of Irish Art from the eighth and ninth centuries AD, over eight hundred years after the Iron Age.

2017 Higher Level paper: Section I, Question 2

Name, describe and discuss the two artefacts [the Clones Fibula and the Broighter Collar] illustrated on the accompanying sheet. In your answer refer to form, function, materials and the techniques used in their production and decoration.

and

Briefly describe and discuss the periods in which these artefacts were made.

Illustrate your answer.

2015 Higher Level paper: Section I, Question 1

'The "Petrie Crown" illustrated on the accompanying sheet is an example of a remarkable change in style that took place during the Iron Age.'

Discuss this statement referring to the function, form, and style of the Petrie Crown, and to the materials and techniques used in its production and decoration.

and

Name and describe one example of decorative stone carving from this period.

Illustrate your answer.

Marking scheme

Q.		Marks	Notes
A	Discussion of statement	10	5 for naming La Tène 5 for discussion
B	Discussion of Petrie Crown with reference to function, form, style and to the materials and techniques used in its production and decoration	20	
C	Name and description of one example of decorative stone carving from this period	15	5 for named artefact 10 for description
D	Sketches	5	
	Total	50	

Discuss the statement!

When a question asks you to discuss the statement it is very important that your answer should focus on this. The students' first response does not fully address the point. Compare this to the second introductory paragraph where the emphasis is on the changes and how this affected art.

SAMPLE QUESTION

'The Iron Age in Ireland saw a change in the design and decoration of metal objects and stone carving.'

Discuss this statement making reference to one named example of metalwork and one named example of stone carving of the period.

and

Discuss briefly the influence of the La Tène style on later Irish art of the Early Christian Period.

Use sketches to illustrate your answer.

Marking scheme

Q.		Marks
A	Discussion of statement with reference to the change in design and decoration in the Iron Age	5
B	Discussion of named metal work object	15
C	Discussion of named stone carving	15
D	Brief discussion of the influence of the La Tène style on later Irish art of the Early Christian Period	5
E	Sketches	10
	Total	**50**

SAMPLE ANSWER

Introduction

Not much is known exactly when and how the Celts came to be in Ireland. The Celts, or kelta as the Greeks and Romans called them, populated much of Europe at around 700 BC. Some believe that they came to Ireland from England by boat. With them they brought a style of art known as La Tène after a site at Lake Neuchâtel in Switzerland. This style combined leafy palmate forms with vines, tendrils, spirals and s-scrolls. They used this in an abstract style to decorate ornaments and weapons. This was a very modern style of design when compared to the basic geometric shapes of the Bronze Age.

The student rewrote the beginning below using the same introductory sentence but made sure in the next paragraph to include information that emphasised 'the

changes in style in metal objects and stone carving' as part of the discussion of the statement.

Answer

Not much is known about exactly when and how the Celts came to be in Ireland. The Celts, or kelta as the Greeks and Romans called them, populated much of Europe at around 700 BC. Some believe that they came to Ireland from England by boat.

The Celtic era is also known as the Iron Age because one of the changes the Celts brought was the use of iron. This was used to make swords, weapons and tools. Many defensive forts were built in the Iron Age Period. Dún Aengus on Inis Mór in the Aran Islands is one of the most famous, but the main evidence of the Celts in Ireland comes from their art. The changes in the design and decoration of metal objects and stone carving during the Iron Age is the most compelling evidence that some of the Celtic people came here.

Celtic art is known as La Tène after a site on the shores of Lake Neuchâtel in Switzerland, where a large number of ornaments and weapons were found in the lake. They were possibly placed there as part of ritual, and a very unique abstract style was used to decorate these objects. This features a combination of leafy palmate forms with vines, tendrils, spirals and s-scrolls.

The La Tène style was evident in Ireland by the third century BC. This very modern style was a huge change in design from the basic geometric shapes that had been used during the Bronze Age and Stone Age. The style is found in several dressed (cut into shape) and decorated stones, mainly found in the north and west of the country. The Turoe Stone in Co. Galway is the largest and the most famous.

Some of the old Bronze Age metal techniques of hammering and cutting were still used during the Iron Age, but casting was greatly improved, while chasing replaced repoussé for relief work. Soldering the surfaces together was also used instead of the Bronze Age method of twisting edges over each other. Bronze continued to be used for decorative work, which can be seen in examples like the Petrie Crown, but the finest decorative pieces of this age were produced in gold. The Broighter Collar is the best example of this.

The Broighter Hoard

A collection or hoard of gold objects was turned up while ploughing a field in Broighter, Co. Derry, and includes some of the finest examples of the goldsmith's art. As well as a very beautiful collar, the hoard also had a model boat with very delicate tiny oars, a bowl made from a thin sheet of gold, two gold chains and two twisted bracelets.

The gold collar from Broighter, Co. Derry

Form

Two tubes are the main element of the collar. They are made from a sheet of gold, with a foliage pattern chased onto the surface. Buffers form a sort of catch at one end. A T-shaped bar is used as a lock that holds the two terminals together. The other terminal, which would have joined the other end, is now missing.

Function

Elaborate collars like this were high-status items worn around the necks of important people on important occasions.

Decoration

The pattern is symmetrical, based on interconnecting s-scrolls. It combines many plant-based forms ending in spiral bosses. The background area between the raised patterns has been chased and

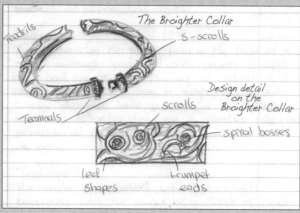

Broigher Collar details

incised with compass marks to create a contrast between the smooth surface and the raised design. On the terminals there is a raised pattern made of lentoids (a kind of circle convex shape) and hollowed bosses with a little gold bead in the centre where it meets the tubes.

Technique

The design would have been applied to a flat gold sheet which was raised by chasing, i.e. pressing back the surrounding surface by hammering. The patterned gold sheets were then heated and rolled into tubes which were soldered, cut and filled with hot mastic (a kind of wax) so tubes could be curved without tearing or crushing them. The buffer terminals were riveted onto the end of the tubes and a row of beading was raised along the edge to disguise the rivet heads.

The Turoe Stone

The Turoe Stone in Co. Galway is the clearest evidence we have that the Celts came to Ireland. This is because the huge stone was far too big to have been brought here and it is local stone so it must have been carved at the location. It is dated to about 50 BC and covered with La Téne-style decoration. The carved decoration shows the very significant changes in the design that took place during the Iron Age, compared to the geometric and curvilinear styles of the Neolithic Period as seen in the very famous decorated stones of Newgrange and Knowth.

Form

This is a four-tonne boulder, 1.68 m tall, made from pink feldspar Galway granite.

Function

The purpose is not really known. It was possibly used as a boundary marker or as a ceremonial object.

Decoration

The decoration completely covers the dome shape in a semi-abstract pattern of leaf and vines, with shapes, trumpet ends and spirals all flowing in a casual symmetry. The spaces between the raised shapes of the lines and whirls also form part of the overall design. The

The Turoe Stone

design has four separate segments for each of the four sides: two semicircular designs take up most of the stone's area, and between these are two smaller triangular segments of pattern that connect over the top of the stone. A single triskele appears at the top of one of the segments, and a brick or step pattern forms a band all

Turoe Stone designs

around the end of the dome that separates it from the plain base.

Technique

The stone was carved with iron chisels. The background was cut away to a depth of about 3 mm, leaving a pattern standing in low relief.

The influence of the Early Christian Period on later Irish art

Many elements of the La Tène style were incorporated into Irish art styles well into the Early Christian Period from the fifth to the twelfth centuries. Motifs such as the tendrils, s-scrolls, spirals and whirls can be seen in the decoration of stone crosses and metal objects like the Crosses at Ahenny, the Tara Brooch and the Ardagh Chalice. The influence is also very significant in manuscripts such as the richly decorated carpet pages of the Book of Durrow, but the influence of the La Tène style can be seen especially in the Rinnegan Crucifixion Plaque.

The Rinnegan Crucifixion Plaque

This little object from the eighth century, which was probably originally attached to a book, shows a crucifixion scene. The figure of Christ, as well as the angels sitting on each of his shoulders and the two figures at his side, are decorated with a La Téne-like design that includes spirals based on triskeles, as well as interlace.

R. O'Driscoll, 2017

3 Early Christian Ireland

Christianity in Ireland

Saint Patrick came to Ireland in AD 432. This date traditionally marks Ireland's move to Christianity.

Early Christian art in Ireland

- The establishment of Christianity in Ireland marks the beginning of a great period in Irish art.
- Christianity and Roman learning combined to create a dynamic force.
- Roman influence is found in the design of jewellery and manuscripts.

Phases in art in Early Christian Ireland

Phase 1: Fifth to eighth century

- Early monastic settlements.

Phase 2: Eighth and ninth centuries: the 'Golden Age' of Irish Art

- Manuscripts.
- Metalwork.
- Carved stone crosses.

Phase 3: Eleventh and twelfth centuries

- Revival of craftsmanship.
- Magnificent shrines for relics.

St Patrick and other missionaries established small communities ruled by their own bishop, but in the two centuries that followed, there was a gradual shift towards monastic settlements. This made Church organisations in Ireland very different from that of Britain or continental Europe.

Architecture in Early Christian Ireland

Example	Location	Function	Date
Skellig Michael	Island off the coast of Co. Kerry.	Monastic settlement.	Sixth to eighth century.
Gallarus Oratory	Dingle Peninsula.	Place of worship.	Eighth or ninth century.
Round towers	Clonmacnoise, Co. Offaly. Glendalough, Co. Wicklow. Monasterboice, Co. Louth. Ardmore, Co. Waterford.	Storing valuables. Places of refuge.	Tenth century.

Monasticism in Ireland

Irish Celtic society was based on kinship and tribes. There were no towns or roads, so Christianity was organised in quite a different way to Rome or Europe because it had to suit the rural make-up of society. It was adapted and blended with pre-Christian traditions.

The founders of early Irish monasteries were considered saints. The monasteries, burial places and relics associated with these saints became centres of pilgrimage. Some of the best known are:

- St Kevin of Glendalough.
- St Enda of Aran.
- St Ciaran of Clonmacnoise.
- St Brigid of Kildare.

The monasteries

Monasteries became of great economic importance in the community. Christianity had brought literacy to Ireland so they became centres of learning. They were also places of refuge for pilgrims, the sick, widows and orphans.

They grew and developed over the seventh and eighth centuries, and the simple austerity of the early monasteries was replaced by the wealth and power of large, well-organised establishments.

The Golden Age of Irish art

As monastic life flourished in the eighth century, Ireland became the cultural, educational and craft centre of Europe. The monks and craftworkers produced magnificent handwritten manuscripts, chalices, crosses, jewellery and many other articles in gold and silver.

Influences on Irish design

Outside influences mixed with Celtic design, and this evolved into a unique Irish style found on all the crafts:

- Spirals and pelta shapes were adapted from the native Celtic design.
- Interlace was of Middle Eastern origin. This probably came to Ireland via the Mediterranean countries and Rome.
- Animal ornament was of Germanic origin, but the influence of Anglo-Saxon sources in Northumbria brought it to Ireland.

Manuscripts

Beautiful handwritten and illuminated (painted) books were produced in the monasteries.

St Colmcille (also called St Columba) and his followers are particularly associated with manuscript production. He established monasteries in Durrow, Co. Offaly, Derry and Iona off the west coast of Scotland.

Book	Decoration	Function
The Cathach, c. AD 600	Black and white, with a small amount of red and yellow. Confined to the first letter of each paragraph. Old Celtic motifs adapted from metalwork. Stylised animal ornament.	Used as a prayer book. Also used as a battle cry and a protector. Before going into battle, a chosen monk would place the book around his neck and walk three times around the troops.
Book of Durrow, c. AD 650	Irish majuscule script. Pages decorated in red, yellow, green and deep brown against a background of black or the plain vellum page. Ornamented 'carpet pages' contain: • La Tène motifs, including spirals and triskeles. • Animal ornament and interlaced beasts.	Probably intended for use on an altar, as it is too large to be carried around easily.

Book of Kells, c. AD 800	New features include:	May have been made to commemorate the centenary of the death of Colmcille (AD 597).
	• Animal drawings between the lines of text. • New colours. • Figurative scenes.	

Script and decoration

The first Irish manuscripts are written in the distinctively Irish 'half-uncial' script.

Small books were written in the 'miniscule' script and large manuscripts were written in the solemn, 'majuscule' script and illuminated (painted) in colour. These were for use on the altar on special occasions.

From the seventh to the ninth centuries, manuscripts became more elaborate. These were masterpieces of calligraphy and more beautiful than anything in the rest of Europe. They were produced in a room of the monastery called a scriptorium and to protect them they were hung in leather satchels on the walls.

Materials

- **Vellum** (writing parchment) was made from calfskin.
- **Colours** were often imported from abroad.

Books were sometimes stored in ornate gold or silver boxes (shrines) encrusted with jewels and precious stones. These materials were very expensive so the monasteries producing manuscripts had to be very wealthy and needed a large herd of calves.

The Cathach: Sixth century

The Cathach is the oldest Irish illuminated manuscript. The word means 'battle book' and refers to one of the earliest copyright disputes.

St Colmcille copied a valuable book lent to him by St Finnian and there was disagreement about ownership. The King of Tara ruled in a very famous judgment: 'To every cow her calf, so to every book its copy', but the dispute ended with a battle that claimed the lives of 3,000 men. As penance, St Colmcille was exiled to Iona.

Celtic motifs adapted from metalwork includes stylised animal ornament

Decorative first letters of opening paragraphs

Most letters are black and white but some have small areas of red

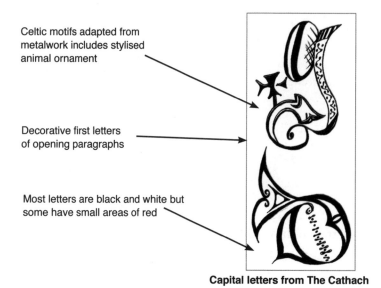

Capital letters from The Cathach

The Book of Durrow: late seventh century

Evangelist page – The Lion of St John

The Book of Durrow does not use the traditional scheme of Evangelist symbols. Instead the lion is used for John and not the eagle.

Decoration

The focus of the decoration was on the Carpet Pages and the Evangelists' symbols. It was decorated in red, yellow, green and deep brown against a background of black or the plain vellum page, and was one of the first books to feature stylised beasts.

Carpet page (folio 191v)

An elaborately ornamented page follows each of the Evangelist pages.

Function

It was probably intended for use on an altar, as it is too large to be carried around easily

Before each gospel, there is a symbol of the Evangelist in Celtic ornamental style

Large areas of undecorated space

Animal ornament and interlaced beasts

La Tène motifs, including spirals and triskeles

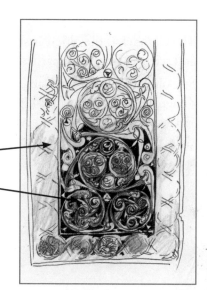

The Book of Kells: c. AD 800

The Book of Kells is the most famous of all Irish manuscripts. It contains the four gospels and is written in the Irish majuscule script. There are 680 pages and many are very elaborately decorated.

The book may have commemorated the centenary of the death of Colmcille (AD 597) and was written around the time the monks left Iona to found the new Columban monastery of Kells.

Colours

Five main colours are used in the Book of Kells:

> **key point**
>
> No gold was used in the Book of Kells, although gold leaf was commonly used in manuscripts of the time. Ultramarine blue was the most expensive colour, due to the scarcity of lapis lazuli, which is found only in the Himalayas.

- Red was made from red lead and it has kept its brightness very well.
- Yellow was made from egg white and a mineral called orpiment. This colour has a shiny surface and looks like gold.
- Green was made from copper and it has an emerald colour.
- Purple probably came from a Mediterranean leaf and was imported into Ireland.
- Blue came from the precious stone called lapis lazuli.

Artists

The four main artists on the Book of Kells have been named as follows.

- **The Illustrator**: Responsible for the Virgin and Child; the Arrest of Christ; and the Temptation.
- **The Portraitist**: Responsible for the portraits of Christ, Matthew and John.
- **The Goldsmith**: Responsible for the fine pages introducing the four gospels and the Chi-Rho page.
- **The Second Master**: Responsible for the cats and kittens on the end of the Chi-Rho page and the charming depictions of animals and everyday life found in the margins and between the lines.

The Chi-Rho symbol

> **key point**
>
> **The Chi-Rho symbol** is a combination of the first two letters of the word 'Christ' in Greek: the Chi (CH) and the Rho (R). In Roman and Medieval times, these two letters written together stood for Christianity.

The Chi-Rho page

This is the last and finest page of the Book of Kells . Golden yellow is the most dominant colour.

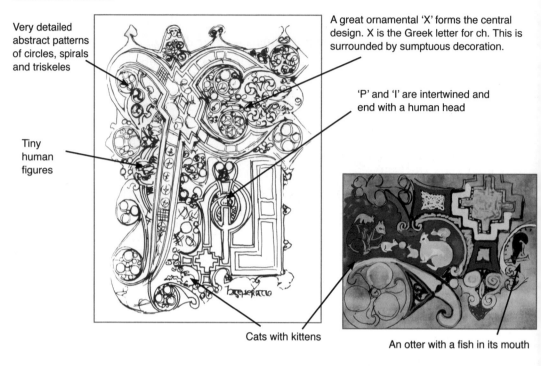

Very detailed abstract patterns of circles, spirals and triskeles

A great ornamental 'X' forms the central design. X is the Greek letter for ch. This is surrounded by sumptuous decoration.

'P' and 'I' are intertwined and end with a human head

Tiny human figures

Cats with kittens

An otter with a fish in its mouth

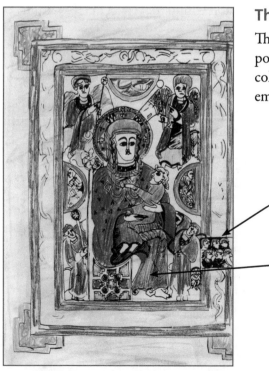

The Birth of Christ

This is a Christmas page. Mary and Jesus are portrayed in a solemn, stylised manner. The colours include several shades of purple and emerald green.

Six human figures, representing the people that Christ came on earth to save

Purple, symbolising royalty

The Arrest of Jesus

Jesus is grabbed by two figures but looks calm and solemn, with arms outstretched in surrender.

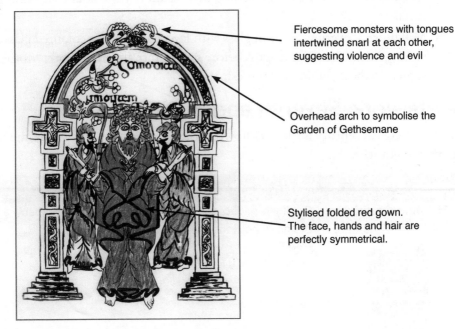

Fiercesome monsters with tongues intertwined snarl at each other, suggesting violence and evil

Overhead arch to symbolise the Garden of Gethsemane

Stylised folded red gown. The face, hands and hair are perfectly symmetrical.

Metalwork: Eight to twelfth centuries

Artistic influences

Colmcille's monastery in Iona brought about links between Britain and Ireland. Anglo-Saxon artistic traditions were passed on to Irish artists and these blended with the earlier La Tène to form a unique style of art in Ireland.

- Solid silver was used for making objects like chalices.
- Enamel was used more frequently.
- A new glasswork technique called millefiori was adopted.
- New objects like large pins and penannular brooches for fastening garments became fashionable.
- Penannular brooches were so called because of the gap in the ring. They were developed from a Roman military-style brooch found in northern Britain.

Eighth-century metalworking techniques

- **Gold filigree**: Patterns made with delicately twisted gold threads.
- **Gilding and silvering**: Covering with a very thin layer of silver or gold.
- **Kerbschnitt**: Also called 'chip carving'; a method of casting that imitates wood carving.
- **Diestamping**: Shaping or cutting metal with a precision tool or die.

- **Enamel:** Glass crushed to a powder and placed in a mould before heating it to an extremely high temperature to make it liquid. It dries to a high-gloss finish.
- **Cloisonné:** A method of enamelling that separates the colours with thin strips of metal.
- **Millefiori:** Covering a cane of glass with layers of different coloured glass and cutting them into short lengths before setting into the metalwork. Motifs are similar to those found in manuscripts.

Metalwork: Seventh and eighth century

The early eighth century is the era known as the 'Golden Age' and was a time of perfection in Irish art.

Object	Materials and Decoration	Function
St John's Crucifixion Plaque Rinnegan	Originally gilded over Bronze. Design of herringbone pattern, spirals and zigzags. Design on the garments in La Tène style.	Probably a book cover.
The Ardagh Chalice 8th Century	The cup and stem are of solid silver, and the rich decoration includes interlace, scrolls, plaits and frets in gold wire filigree. Engraving, casting, enamelling and cloisonné. Coloured glass and a cloisonné enamelled studs.	For use on an altar during religious services.
The Tara Brooch 8th Century	Very detailed decoration on the front and back.	Probably made for the personal adornment of a queen or king.
The Derrynaflan Chalice	Similar decoration to the Ardagh Chalice with filigree, enamelling, casting, engraving, stamping of thin gold, knitted wire mesh, cast glass studs and filigree gold animal interlace.	For use on an altar during religious services.

Rinnegan Crucifixion Plaque

Found at Rinnegan, Co. Roscommon, this dates from the late seventh century and is one of the earliest examples of the crucifixion scene. The figure of Christ is similar to the stone cross at Carndonagh, Co. Donegal.

Form

A small bronze plaque

Function

Numerous small holes suggest it was pinned to wood and was probably a book cover

Decoration

The bronze was originally gilded (covered in a light film of gold)

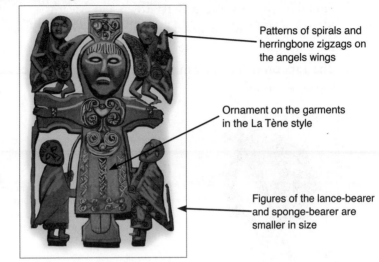

Patterns of spirals and herringbone zigzags on the angels wings

Ornament on the garments in the La Tène style

Figures of the lance-bearer and sponge-bearer are smaller in size

Ardagh Chalice

The Ardagh Chalice dates from the eighth century. It was found by a boy digging potatoes near Ardagh, Co. Limerick in 1868.

Band of gold filigree and red and blue glass studs

A cross within a roundel is richly decorated with spirals of gold wire filigree work and coloured glass

Cloisonné-enamelled stud

Gilding over bronze on the stem

Cast gold collar decorated in high relief

Handles on both sides decorated with coloured glass panels and gold filigree work

The names of all the apostles except Judas are engraved lightly into the silver

Square blocks of blue glass separated by panels of interlace and geometric ornament

Form

A mounded chalice with handles is joined to a base by a thick bronze stem. A cone-shaped foot gives it extra stability.

Metalworking technique

The bowl of the chalice is made of silver, and the sumptuous decoration is offset by the plain areas of metal

Decoration

Interlace, animal interlace, scrolls, plaits and frets in gold wire filigree, as well as engraving, casting, enamelling and cloisonné. In the centre of the underside of the base is a circular crystal surrounded by gold filigree and green enamels.

Tara Brooch

- Dates from the eighth century.
- It is a penannular brooch. Pennanular brooches were based on a Roman design.
- Found on the seashore at Bettystown, Co. Meath. Nearby, a cliff had collapsed because of sea erosion. A jeweller who had the brooch for some time named it the 'Tara Brooch' and the name has remained.
- The Tara Brooch is close in style to the Ardagh Chalice and may have come from the same workshop.

> **key point**
>
> The Tara Brooch displays every skill available to the metalworker of the time.

Function

Probably made for the personal adornment of a queen or king

Form

A ring brooch with no gap through which the pin can pass. This makes it a pseudo-penannular brooch. A cain and loops make up the fastening. The mesh chain suggests it may have been one of a pair originally joined together across the back of the shoulders.

Decoration

The brooch is crowded with detailed decoration on the front and back. An astonishing amount of minutely detailed ornamentation fits into a very small space.

Decoration on the head of the pin

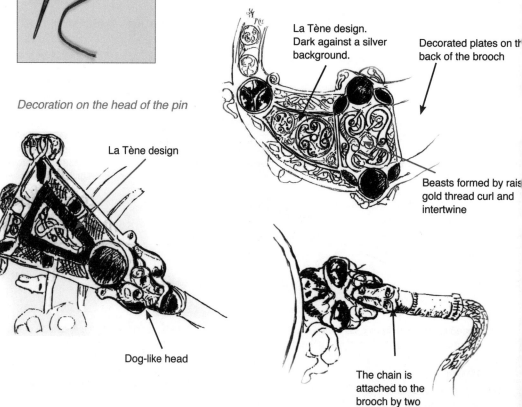

La Tène design. Dark against a silver background.

Decorated plates on the back of the brooch

La Tène design

Beasts formed by raised gold thread curl and intertwine

Dog-like head

The chain is attached to the brooch by two animal heads

Derrynaflan Hoard

A hoard of liturgical items dating from the eighth century, including a chalice, a silver paten and a beautiful strainer-ladle were found at the ancient monastery of Derrynaflan, Co. Tipperary.

Derrynaflan Chalice

Closely related to the Ardagh Chalice, with similar decoration.

Decoration

- Filigree, enamelling, casting, engraving, stamping of thin gold and knitting of wire mesh.
- Cast glass studs, filigree gold animal interlace, engraving and knitted wire mesh surround the edges.

2016 Ordinary Level paper: Section I, Question 3

The 'Ardagh Chalice', illustrated on the accompanying sheet, is an example of Irish Christian metalwork.

Answer (a), (b) and (c).

(a) What was its function?

(b) Describe and discuss how it was made and decorated.

(c) Name and briefly describe and discuss one other metal artefact from this period.

Illustrate your answer.

Marking scheme

Q. 3		Marks	Notes
A	Function	10	
B	Description and discussion on how it was made and decorated	20	
C	Name, description and discussion of one other metal artefact from this period	15	5 for name 10 for discussion
D	Sketches	5	
	Total	**50**	

2016 Higher Level paper: Section I, Question 2

'The Book of Kells, containing the four gospels in Latin, is celebrated for its intricate design and lavish decoration.'

Discuss this statement with reference to the illustration on the accompanying sheet. In your answer name the page and refer to design, ornamentation, imagery and how the book was produced.

and

Name and briefly describe and discuss one other Irish manuscript that you have studied.

Illustrate your answer.

Marking scheme

Q.2		Marks	Notes
A	Discussion of statement and name of illustrated page	10	7 for discussion of statement 3 for name of page
B	Description and discussion of the illustrated page with reference to design, ornamentation and imagery	10	
C	Description and discussion of how the book was produced	10	
D	Name and brief description and discussion of one other Irish manuscript you have studied	15	5 for name 10 for description and discussion
E	Sketches	5	
	Total	**50**	

Metalwork: eleventh and twelfth centuries

Artistic production in Ireland declined considerably during the late eighth and ninth centuries. However, the eleventh and twelfth centuries saw a great revival in craftsmanship. Stoneworkers and metalworkers produced works of art that equalled, if not outshone, the masterpieces of the earlier years.

Almost all the fine metalwork of this period is associated with the Church and great care was taken in the creation and decoration of sacred objects like:

- Ornamented shrines for books.
- Reliquaries connected with relics of early Irish saints.
- Croziers.

Patrons

The scale of production and the craftsmanship involved show that the arts were patronised by well-to-do clans and royalty of the time.

Scandinavian influence

One of the most notable features of the metalwork is the blend of Scandinavian influences with native Irish work. This is seen particularly in the use of animal imagery.

Examples

- Shrine of St Lactin's Arm may have been made to hold the bones of a saint.
- Book shrine of the Cathach.
- Shrine of St Patrick's Bell.
- Cross of Cong.
- Lismore Crozier.

Cross of Cong

Turlough Mór O'Connor, King of Connaught, had a fragment of the True Cross. The Cross of Cong was the shrine made for this precious relic. It is one of Ireland's most important shrines.

Cross of Cong

Function

- A processional cross made to enshrine a fragment of the True Cross.
- The relic is protected by a crystal rock set in a silver mount and surrounded by gold filigree in the centre of the cross.

Decoration

- Tubular silver edging surrounds the curved outline of the cross.
- The cross surface is divided into ornamented sections of cast bronze thread-like snakes holding animal shapes.
- The staff and the cross are linked together by animal jaws biting the base of the cross.
- These animals have scaled heads, pointed ribbed snouts, little curved ears and blue glass eyes.

Stone carving in Ireland

Pre-Christian

Entrance stone, Newgrange, Co. Meath	Standing stones	Stone circles, Co. Kerry	Turoe Stone, Co. Galway	Castlestrange Stone, Co. Roscommon

Early Christian (Sixth to Eighth Century)

Reask Pillar, Co. Kerry	Aglish Pillar, Co. Kerry

Carved Crosses (Seventh Century)

Carndonagh Cross, Co. Donegal	Fahan Mura, Co. Donegal

High Crosses (Eighth Century)
Crosses at Ahenny, Co. Tipperary

North

South

Crosses of the Scriptures (Ninth Century)

Cross of Moone, Co. Kildare

Cross of Muireadach, Co. Louth

Eleventh- and Twelfth-Century Crosses

Dysart O'Dea Cross, Co. Clare

Kilfenora Cross, Co. Clare

Stone carving in Pre-Christian times was done by cutting stone into slabs and standing stones. The tradition continued into early Christian times and Christian symbols began to appear along with the traditional ogham writing on standing stones. Legend has it that there was a fear in pre-Christian Ireland that carving the stone itself might interfere with the 'spirit' of the stone.

Stone carving on Irish crosses:

- Free-standing: seventh century.
- Ringed crosses: eighth century.
- Tall crosses of the scriptures: ninth and tenth centuries.

High Cross art

Carved crosses were made from sandstone, granite or limestone, and featured several panels filled with carvings. The decoration was both abstract and figurative. It was highly stylised.

Abstract carvings

These comprise Celtic spiral or interlace designs:

- Zoomorphic (animal-shaped) motifs.
- Knotwork.
- Mazes.
- Labyrinths.
- Key patterns.

Figurative carvings

- Bible scenes from the Old and New Testaments.
- The crucifixion.
- Resurrection of Christ.

Characteristics of the Celtic High Crosses

The basic components of the Celtic High Cross are:

- Base.
- Shaft.
- Ring.
- Capstone.
- Sculpture panels.

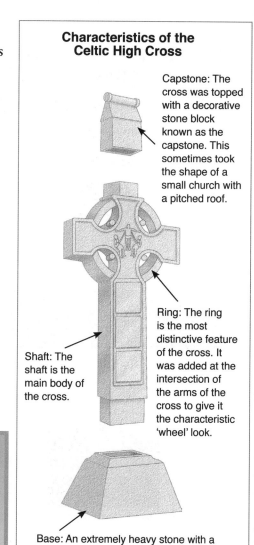

Characteristics of the Celtic High Cross

Capstone: The cross was topped with a decorative stone block known as the capstone. This sometimes took the shape of a small church with a pitched roof.

Ring: The ring is the most distinctive feature of the cross. It was added at the intersection of the arms of the cross to give it the characteristic 'wheel' look.

Shaft: The shaft is the main body of the cross.

Base: An extremely heavy stone with a socket forms the base, and the cross is placed into this by means of a tenon.

Function of High Crosses

- It is not known exactly what function High Crosses served.
- They may have been boundary markers or monuments close to monasteries, but the scenes from the Bible also probably served as lessons because very few people could read and write. For this reason the High Crosses of Ireland have been called 'sermons in stone'.
- Biblical scenes may have served as lessons.
- High Crosses have been called 'sermons in stone' because most people of the time could not read and might have used the High Crosses for spiritual learning.

Cross-inscribed stones

Grave slabs

Large numbers of engraved grave slabs are found near monasteries. They show cross designs and inscriptions.

Free-standing stones

- **Duvillaun Slab**, Co. Mayo: Greek cross with an early representation of the crucifixion.
- **Reask Pillar**, Co. Kerry: Carved Maltese cross with Celtic decoration.
- **Aglish Pillar**, Co. Kerry: Interesting combination of ogham and a Greek cross.

key point

Visit www.highcrosses.org for detailed pictures of a wide selection of Ireland's High Crosses.

Seventh-century crosses

Carndonagh Cross

This was the first free-standing stone cross and the first cut in a cruciform.

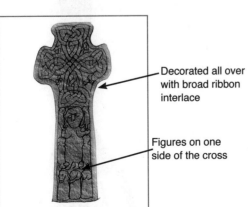

Decorated all over with broad ribbon interlace

Figures on one side of the cross

Fahan Mura Slab

This is the only cross in early Irish art that has an inscription. It is written in Greek.

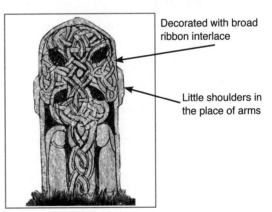

Decorated with broad ribbon interlace

Little shoulders in the place of arms

Eighth-century crosses: Crosses at Ahenny

Two highly-ornamented crosses are found a few metres apart and at Ahenny, Co. Tipperary.

Ahenny North   **Ahenny South**

Decoration

Mainly abstract ornament, similar to metalwork of the time. Rounded bosses at the joints have no function in stone. This suggests that it might have been inspired by an object in metal. High-relief rope mouldings is a distinctive feature around the edges of the ring and cross.

Form

The crosses are quite short with a widely spaced ring and a wide base. A large portion of the shaft is above the ring. The north cross has an unusual conical-shaped cap.

Crosses of the Scriptures: Ninth and tenth centuries

Crosses of the Scriptures are decorated with panels of Bible stories that were popular lessons at the time.

Cross of Moone

This tall, slender cross is made of granite. It is tapering and elegant in shape and the ring is quite narrow. The capstone is missing. The base is a tall rectangle with four even sides covered with carved figures.

Decoration

This was one of the earliest crosses to introduce biblical scenes

Panels depict scenes from the Old and New Testaments

The figures are square-shaped and abstract

Figurative scenes

Biblical scenes on the sides of the base show how God intervenes to save the good.

This is the most famous scene on the cross. Figures with square bodies and large staring eyes fill the panel in three neat rows.

The twelve apostles

The east side of the base

Daniel in the lion's den

The west side of the base

The flight of the holy family into Egypt

The miracle of the loaves and fishes

The north side of the base

key point

Visit www.sacred-destinations.com/ireland for excellent information and photos of Muiredach's Cross.

Muiredach's Cross

This is one of the largest and best-preserved High Crosses. It gets its name from an inscription on the base.

Decoration

All the carving is executed in bold rounded relief and is quite realistic

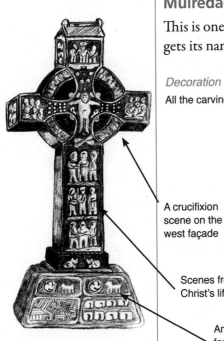

A crucifixion scene on the west façade

Scenes from Christ's life

The arrest of Christ

Two figures grab Christ. Christ's cloak is tied with a pin similar to the Tara Brooch. This denotes his royal status.

Two cats carved in high relief

An inscription in Irish that translates: 'A prayer for Muireadach for whom the cross was made.' Muireadach is thought to be an abbot who died in 922.

Twelfth-century crosses

- A completely different style of cross appeared around the twelfth century. These crosses show much less intricate stone carving.
- The ringed wheel-head was no longer a feature.
- Instead, a simple figure, usually Christ or a bishop, was placed in a prominent position on the upper part of the cross.

Example

Dysart O'Dea Cross, Co. Clare

Dysart O'Dea Cross, Co. Clare

2016 Higher Level paper: Section I, Question 3

'The style of carving on the Cross of Moone, Co. Kildare, contrasts significantly with the style of carving found on the Cross of Muiredach, Monasterboice, Co. Louth.'

Discuss this statement with reference to the illustrations on the accompanying sheet. In your answer refer to form, structure, imagery, decoration and stone-working techniques.

and

Briefly describe and discuss the functions of Irish High Crosses.

Illustrate your answer.

Marking scheme

Q.3		Marks
A	Discussion of statement; significant contrasting styles of carving	5
B	Description and discussion of Cross of Moone under form, structure, imagery, decoration and stone-working techniques	15
C	Description and discussion of Cross of Muiredach under form, structure, imagery, decoration and stone-working techniques	15
D	Briefly describe and discuss the functions of Irish High Crosses	10
E	Sketches	5
	Total	50

Architecture in Eighteenth-Century Georgian Ireland

 aims

- Gain knowledge of the dominant Classical architectural style of the period
- Recognise and name the architectural and decorative features of the buildings
- Identify the functional and aesthetic qualities of the materials used in the exteriors and interiors
- Understand the concept of public buildings
- Identify the relationships between architecture and society
- Study original buildings
- Become familiar with appropriate terms

The eighteenth century was a time of **peace and prosperity** in Ireland. A frenzy of building spread throughout the country as the wealthy ascendancy competed to construct elaborate town and country houses. Public buildings were the most beautiful the country had ever seen, and craftsmen of all kinds came from Europe to work in Ireland.

 key point

Eighteenth-century architecture is normally referred to as Georgian. It is named after four kings of England called George, who reigned in succession from 1714 until 1830.

 **exam focus**

The amount of material needed for examination purposes can be studied without difficulty. If you are familiar with Dublin, this is a particularly good study area to choose for the exam.

Georgian Dublin

- Dublin is one of the finest Georgian cities in Europe.
- Dublin was very prosperous in the eighteenth century, with its own parliament largely controlled by the wealthy ascendancy.
- In 1800, the Act of Union abolished the Irish Parliament in Dublin.
- Dublin began to slide into decay and many fine Georgian houses were split up into tenements.

 key point

Take a tour

Many important Georgian buildings in or around Dublin are open to the public and some offer excellent and informative tours.

Georgian architecture

Architecture in the eighteenth century had high ideals. Aesthetic qualities of beauty, proportion and harmony were greatly sought after. The style was influenced by Classicism, which originated in Greece and Rome. This classical style became popular in England and later spread to Ireland.

In order to fully appreciate Georgian Dublin, you should visit the buildings. However, the book *Dublin: A Grand Tour* by Jacqueline O'Brien with Desmond Guinness is a beautiful publication. Everything you could want in information and pictures is here. Your local library should have a copy.

Classical orders

Classical architecture was composed in a specific manner called an order. It is characterised by the use of columns to support an entablature. The three main styles of column design in Classical orders were called Doric, Ionic and Corinthian.

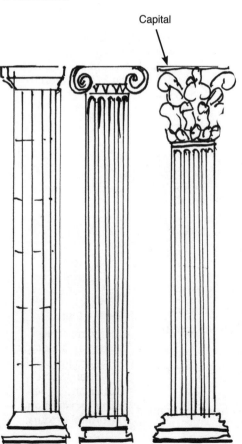

Capital

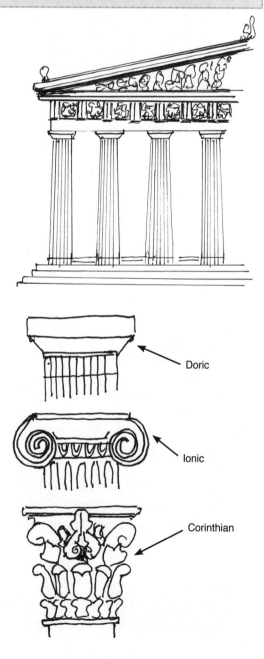

Doric

Ionic

Corinthian

Eighteenth-century architectural styles

- **Palladian**: up to 1760.
- **Neoclassical**: dominant in the late eighteenth and early nineteenth centuries.

Prominent eighteenth-century architects of Irish buildings

- Edward Lovett Pearce (1699–1733): An Irish architect.
- Richard Cassels (1690–1751): A German architect, who later changed his name to Richard Castle.
- William Chambers (1723–1796): A Scottish architect, who never visited Ireland.
- James Gandon (1743–1823): An English architect who trained in the office of William Chambers.

Palladian Period: 1700–1760

Italian Influences

- Andrea Palladio was a sixteenth-century Italian architect.
- He wrote a book based on classical Roman remains.
- The book became the inspiration for a very fashionable style of architecture in England.
- 'Palladianism' first made its appearance in Ireland in large country houses in the eighteenth century.

Country Houses

Castletown House, Co. Kildare	Russborough House, Co. Wicklow	Carton House, Co. Kildare	Westport House, Co. Mayo	Bellamont House, Co. Cavan

Public Buildings

Parliament House (now Bank of Ireland, College Green, Dublin)	Trinity College Dublin	Provost's House, Trinity College

Irish country houses: The Great House

Castletown House, Co. Kildare (1722)

Castletown is the earliest and grandest of Ireland's Palladian country houses. Described as 'the finest house Ireland ever saw', it was designed for William Conolly, speaker of the Irish House of Commons.

Visit www.castletownhouse.ie for a tour of the house and a video of every room.

The central block was designed by Italian architect Alessandro Galilei, and was inspired by Renaissance design

The wings are connected to the house by curved Ionic colonnades (rows of columns)

Irish architect, Sir Edward Lovett Pearce, designed the wings, which were later added to the main house. In true Palladian fashion, these contained the kitchens on one side and the stables on the other.

Interior

The decoration of the Long Galley – the main reception room – was inspired by the excavations at Pompeii at the time of its building. The original hand-painted blue wallpaper remains, and three original glass chandeliers from Venice in blue and pink glass still hang.

Entrance hall

Designed by Edward Lovett Pearce, it consists of two storeys – with Ionic columns and a black-and-white chequered floor. The ornate plasterwork is by the Francini brothers from Italy.

Stairs

The staircase is cantilevered (supported only at the wall). It is made of Portland stone, a pale limestone from Dorset in England.

Russborough House, Co. Wicklow (1741)

Russborough House by Richard Castle is the best-preserved of his Irish country house designs.

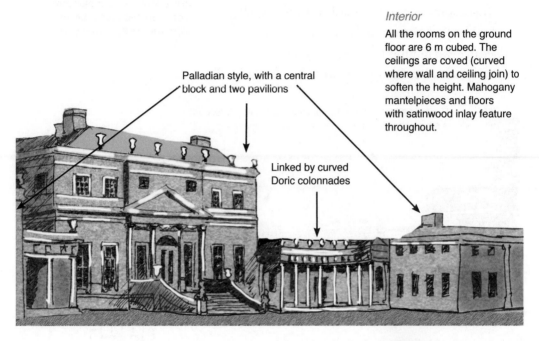

Palladian style, with a central block and two pavilions

Linked by curved Doric colonnades

Interior

All the rooms on the ground floor are 6 m cubed. The ceilings are coved (curved where wall and ceiling join) to soften the height. Mahogany mantelpieces and floors with satinwood inlay feature throughout.

Visit www.russborough.ie for more information.

Public buildings

Trinity College, Dublin

- The college was established by Queen Elizabeth I and Dublin city grew around it.
- A new façade and square were built between 1752 and 1760.
- The new West Front is made of granite with Portland stone columns.
- It has a portico (entrance porch) with six columns in the classical Corinthian style.
- William Chambers designed the Chapel and Public Theatre on either side of the classical Front Square.
- Richard Castle designed the Dining Hall.
- The Provost's House (where the president of the college lives) is one of Dublin's grandest Georgian townhouses.

Parliament House (Bank of Ireland, College Green)

- Parliament House in Dublin was the first purpose-built parliament house in the world.
- It was designed by Sir Edward Lovett Pearce.
- This was the earliest large-scale Palladian public building in Britain or Ireland.
- Pearce did not live to see his most important work completed. He died in 1733 at the age of 34.

key point

Visit www.archiseek.com for a profile and beautiful pictures of Parliament House.

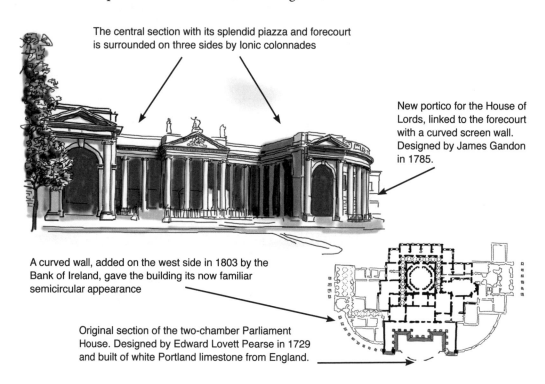

The central section with its splendid piazza and forecourt is surrounded on three sides by Ionic colonnades

New portico for the House of Lords, linked to the forecourt with a curved screen wall. Designed by James Gandon in 1785.

A curved wall, added on the west side in 1803 by the Bank of Ireland, gave the building its now familiar semicircular appearance

Original section of the two-chamber Parliament House. Designed by Edward Lovett Pearse in 1729 and built of white Portland limestone from England.

Townhouses in Dublin

After Richard Castle died in 1751, no architect dominated the building style in late eighteenth-century Dublin. Its character was formed instead by rich and influential families.

Townhouses in Dublin		
Leinster House (1745–1748) Designed by Richard Castle	**Charlemont House, now Municipal Gallery of Art** (1762–1765) Designed by William Chambers	**Casino at Marino** (late 1750s to c. 1775) Designed by William Chambers

Georgian towns

Town planning was particularly concentrated in eighteenth-century England, and Ireland followed suit. Large towns like Dublin saw the development of churches, schools, hospitals and market houses.

Georgian streets and squares

Many Georgian streets still bear the names of the families who developed them. The Fitzwilliam family, Earls of Merrion, developed part of their great estate on the southside of the Liffey in Dublin between 1760 and 1850. The first project was Merrion Street. Fitzwilliam Street, Fitzwilliam Square and Mount Street Upper followed.

Leinster House

- Originally known as Kildare House.
- James Fitzgerald, the Earl of Kildare, built his townhouse on the south side of the river, which was unfashionable at that time.
- Designed by Richard Castle.
- The aim was to have the grandest mansion in all of Dublin to reflect Fitzgerald's eminent position in Irish society.
- On Fitzgerald's appointment to Duke of Leinster in 1766, the house was renamed Leinster House.
- Today Leinster House is the site of the Dáil and Seanad.

Charlemont House

- Charlemont House was originally the townhouse of James Caulfeild, first Earl of Charlemont.
- Caulfield was one of Irelands' great patrons of the arts.
- Charlemont House was designed by William Chambers.
- It became the Municipal Gallery of Modern Art in 1933.

Terraced houses

Dublin's Georgian houses are impressive streetscapes of plain red-bricked terraces. The Wide Streets Commission had the power to impose uniformity on buildings. The house façade, including the spacing and shape of windows, was designed in accordance with classical rules of proportion. Houses were uniform in design and the only variations were in doors, ornate fanlights and balconies.

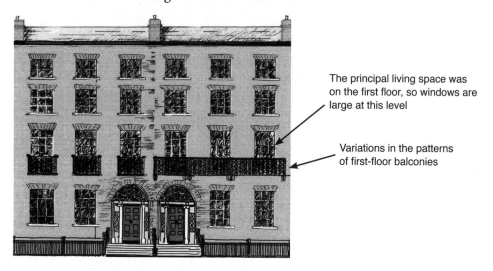

The principal living space was on the first floor, so windows are large at this level

Variations in the patterns of first-floor balconies

Typical Georgian interior

- The richness of Georgian interiors varied according to the wealth of the owner.
- Typically, the fanlight over the main door lit the hallway and led the entrant straight to the stairs and reception rooms on the first floor.
- The hall was paved in stone, often in black and white squares.
- Doors were often surmounted by elaborate over-doors.
- Drawing-room ceilings usually had the most ornate stucco decoration.

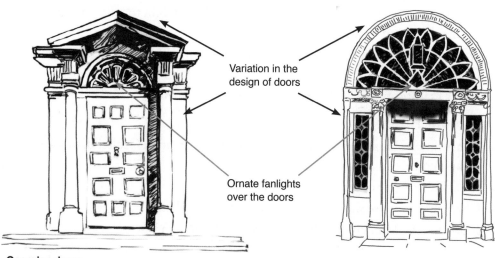

Variation in the design of doors

Ornate fanlights over the doors

Georgian doors

Townhouses outside of Dublin

Limerick

The Pery family has been associated with the city since the seventeenth century. A terrace in Pery Square, Limerick is a fine example of Georgian architecture. Number 2 Pery Square has been fully restored with all its original architectural features expertly reinstated in precise detail. Decor and furnishings are also from the Georgian era.

Pery Square, Limerick

Neoclassical Period: Late eighteenth and early nineteenth centuries

In England, Palladianism was quite suddenly replaced by a purer style based on classical Greek architecture. The change was more gradual in Ireland.

Influences on the style

- Young gentlemen travelled to Italy as part of the 'Grand Tour' and saw ancient Rome for themselves.
- In England a book called *Antiquities of Athens* was published. It was full of drawings of reconstructions of Greek buildings and it became very popular.

Neoclassical buildings in Dublin

- Blue Coat School: designed by Thomas Ivory (1773).
- The Casino at Marino: designed by William Chambers (1760).
- Custom House: designed by James Gandon (1781).
- Four Courts: designed by James Gandon (1786).
- Portico, Parliament House: designed by James Gandon (1785).

Blue Coat School

- The former Blue Coat School is now occupied by the Law Society of Ireland.
- The building is essentially Palladian, but it has some new details, e.g. blank niches on the main floor and windows.
- This marks the beginning of the Neoclassical style.

James Caulfield (Lord Charlemont)

- James Caulfield, first Earl of Charlemont, was one of Ireland's most enlightened and cultivated men.
- Lord Charlemont was well known for his love of classical art and culture.
- He spent nine years on the Grand Tour of Europe, visiting Rome before travelling on to Greece.

- He collected paintings, books and antique sculptures and had them shipped home.
- He befriended many young architects, painters and stuccodores.
- On his return to Ireland, he commissioned William Chambers to design both his townhouse and country house.
- His country house at Marino was destroyed in a fire, but the Casino in the grounds remains intact.

The Casino at Marino: AD 1760

The Casino (meaning small house) probably had very little function but it is a perfect gem of architectural design.

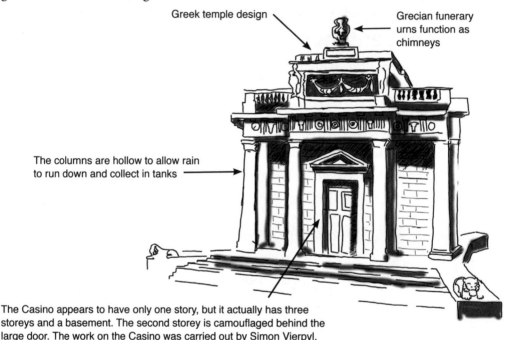

Greek temple design

Grecian funerary urns function as chimneys

The columns are hollow to allow rain to run down and collect in tanks

The Casino appears to have only one story, but it actually has three storeys and a basement. The second storey is camouflaged behind the large door. The work on the Casino was carried out by Simon Vierpyl, following William Chambers' direction.

Custom House, Dublin

- In 1781 James Gandon was summoned to Dublin to build a new Custom House.
- It was built on slob land that was reclaimed from the estuary of the Liffey when the Wide Streets Commissioners constructed the Quays.
- Republican forces burned the Custom House in 1921, and Gandon's original interior was completely destroyed.
- The central dome was rebuilt with native Irish limestone, which is slightly darker than the original Portland stone.
- The best-known carvings are the Riverine heads set in the keystones above the doors and windows, which represent the rivers of Ireland. The Liffey, which appears over the main door, is the only female in the series.

A potico with free-standing Doric columns

The building has four façades, each one different but linked by corner pavilions

Sculptured heads, by Edward Smyth, set in the keystones above the doors and windows, represent the rivers of Ireland

The Liffey, over the main door, is the only female in the riverine head series

The figure is surrounded with the fruits of the countryside that grow in abundance along the riverbanks

The Four Courts

- The Four Courts were also designed by James Gandon.
- The building was damaged in 1922 when it was burned by Free State troops fighting in the Civil War.
- The original façade has been restored, but the interior was lost.

Portico for the House of Lords

- James Gandon designed the large new portico as a separate entrance for the House of Lords at Parliament House.
- Corinthian-style columns are a feature of the portico.

Stucco (plasterwork)

Plasterwork is called 'stucco' work after the Italian word meaning plaster. Stucco was very popular in grand Irish houses, in townhouses and country houses alike. Some very fine stucco is to be found in Irish Georgian houses and the styles changed over the years from 1725 to 1800.

Stuccodores

Paul and Philip La Francini

- The Francini brothers were brought from Italy to Ireland in 1738 by the Earl of Kildare to execute the great saloon ceiling at Carton House, Co. Kildare.
- They introduced the human figure into plasterwork.
- Most of their work is plain white with high-relief figures, flowers and garlands.
- They worked in the Rococo manner, a style fashionable in most of Europe and associated with swirling ornament.
- The work of the Francini brothers profoundly influenced Irish stuccodores.

Robert West

- Robert West was an Irish stuccodore who worked in the Rococo manner.
- He produced some of the finest plasterwork in Dublin.

Robert Adam and Michael Stapleton

- Robert Adam was an English architect and furniture designer who developed a style of plasterwork that became popular in England after the 1760s.
- He used moulds to produce low-relief plasterwork in the Neoclassical style.
- Michael Stapleton inherited Robert West's practice and went on to produce sophisticated, delicate work in the Adams style.
- This kind of plasterwork looks very well picked out in colour.
- Examples of this work can be found in many Dublin buildings, including Trinity College and Lucan House (now the Italian Embassy).

Stucco in Irish country houses

Superb examples of La Francini work can be seen at Carton House, Castletown House and Russborough House. Copies of Francini stucco were taken from Riverstown House, Co. Cork in 1948 and they can be seen in a corridor at Áras an Uachtaráin.

Castletown House

The staircase walls at Castletown House are elaborately decorated with Francini work.

It features shells, garlands, Chinese dragons and masks

Russborough House

- Some of Ireland's finest plasterwork can be found at Russborough House.
- Records of the work were destroyed during the destruction of the Four Courts during the Civil War.
- In the absence of written records, it can only be assumed that stucco on the ceilings of the saloon, library and music room is the work of the Francini brothers.
- The saloon ceiling is filled with garlands of flowers and little putti and the library and stairway are also superbly decorated.

Terraced houses

Magnificent stucco work can be found on the staircases and ceilings of Dublin's terraced houses.

Number 20 Dominick Street

Robert West built number 20 Dominick Street for himself.

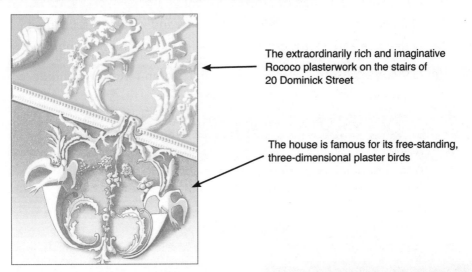

The extraordinarily rich and imaginative Rococo plasterwork on the stairs of 20 Dominick Street

The house is famous for its free-standing, three-dimensional plaster birds

Belvedere House

- Michael Stapleton's delicately modelled stucco can be seen at its imaginative best in Belvedere House.
- The walls and ceilings are covered with a rich display of coloured medallions surrounded by lace-like geometric patterns.
- Colour dominates the stairs, ceiling and walls in blue, yellow and pale green as well as russet.

The walls and ceilings of Belvedere House are covered with a rich display of coloured medallions surrounded by lace-like geometric patterns

2017 Ordinary Level paper: Section II, Question 4

Choose one Georgian building that you have studied and answer (a), (b) and (c).

(a) Name the building and its architect(s).

(b) Describe and discuss your chosen building referring to location and structure.

(c) Briefly describe and discuss one interior decorative feature found in your chosen building.

Illustrate your answer.

2016 Ordinary Level paper: Section II, Question 4

James Gandon (1743–1823) designed public and private buildings in Ireland. Answer (a), (b) and (c).

(a) Name a building designed by James Gandon.

(b) Describe and discuss the architectural features and style of this building.

(c) Briefly describe and discuss one decorative feature of this building.

Illustrate your answer.

Marking scheme

Q. 4		Marks
A	Name	5
B	Description and discussion of the architectural features and style of the building	25
C	Brief description and discussion of one decorative feature of this building	10
D	Sketches	10
	Total	**50**

2016 Higher Level paper: Section II, Question 4

Select one of the following architects:

- Richard Castle (Cassels) (1690–1751)
- William Chambers (1723–1796).

Describe and discuss the architectural features, both structural and decorative, of a named building by your chosen architect.

and

Name and briefly describe and discuss one other building by your chosen architect.

Illustrate your answer.

Marking scheme

Q. 4		Marks	Notes
A	Name of building by your chosen architect	5	
B	Description and discussion of architectural features, both structural and decorative	20	
C	Name and brief description and discussion of one other building by chosen architect	15	5 for name 10 for description and discussion
D	Sketches	10	
	Total	50	

2015 Higher Level paper: Section II, Question 4

The building illustrated on the accompanying sheet was designed by James Gandon (1743–1823).

Answer (a), (b), and (c).

(a) Name the building and describe and discuss how the features of this building are typical of Georgian architecture.

(b) Describe and discuss how sculpture was used to decorate this building.

(c) Name and describe one other public building by this architect.

Illustrate your answer.

Marking scheme

Q. 4		Marks	Notes
A	Name of building and description, and discussion of the features of this building which are typical of Georgian architecture	20	5 for name 15 for description and discussion
B	Description and discussion of how sculpture was used to decorate this building	10	
C	Name and brief description and discussion of **one** other public building by this architect	15	5 for name 10 for description & discussion
D	Sketches	5	
	Total	50	

2017 Higher Level paper: Section II, Question 4

Describe and discuss the architectural features of a named Irish building in the Neoclassical style. Name the architect of your chosen building and refer in your answer to the structure, decoration and layout of both the interior and exterior of the building.

and

Briefly describe and discuss the work of any named stuccodore of this period in Ireland.

Illustrate your answer.

Break down the question

Topic

'An Irish building in the Neoclassical style'

Task words

Describe

Discuss

Details to consider

Architectural features

Structure, decoration and layout

Interior and exterior

What? When? How? Why? Where?

- When did the Neoclassical style become popular in Ireland?
- What ideas influenced and inspired the architects?
- What were its unique architectural features?
- How did the architectural features differ from previous styles?
- Name a building that, in your opinion, is one of the best examples of the style in Ireland?
- Why is this?
- Is this a public building or a private dwelling?
- What are the architectural features of this building?
- Who was the architect?
- Was this architect considered an important figure? Why was that?
- What was the layout of this building – was it small or large?
- What was the layout of the interior?
- How was the building structured?
- How was the exterior decorated?
- How was the interior decorated?

Brief discussion on the work of a named stuccodore:

- Who was the stuccodore?
- In what period and style did they work?
- What features are particularly associated with this work?
- What inspired and influenced the work?
- What work is, in your opinion, the best example of this stuccodore's work?
- Why is this?

Sketches

SAMPLE ANSWER

The Georgian Period was a wonderful time for the art of decoration and architecture in Ireland. An extended period of peace from about 1720 to 1800 resulted in some the most elegant and elaborate architecture the country had ever seen.

Architecture was greatly influenced by sixteenth-century Italian architect Andrea Palladio. He published books that were focused on his work on the classical remains of ancient Rome. A manuscript by the ancient Roman architect Vitruvius was also a guide for some eighteenth-century designs.

Palladianism went out of fashion quite suddenly, and towards the end of the century the Neoclassical style became popular first in England and then in Ireland.

Young men of means took what was known as the 'Grand Tour', travelling around Europe. An important aspect of this was visiting the remains of ancient Rome.

By the end of the eighteenth century, travel to Greece had become possible and a newly published book called *Antiquities of Athens* became the inspiration for a new and more authentic classical style of architecture that included features like columns, triangular pediments and decorative details inspired by ancient Greek temples.

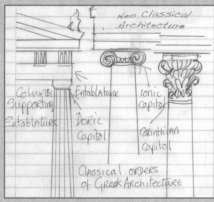

Classical orders of Greek architecture

Lord Charlemont

James Caulfield of Dublin, who later became Earl of Charlemont, went on a nine-year Grand Tour of Rome and Greece as part of his education. He absorbed a great deal of the classical influence and made several important friends, including the young English architect William Chambers, the sculptor Simon Vierpyl and artist and decorator Giovanni Battista Cipriani. On his return to Dublin in 1755, he employed William Chambers to bring the Italian style to both his town and country houses. Chambers himself, however, never visited Ireland so Simon Vierpyl saw that these designs were carried out.

Marino

Lord Charlemont's country house in Donnycarney was called 'Marino' in memory one of the Italian towns he had visited. This house is now demolished but the small villa or garden temple built in the grounds still stands.

The Casino at Marino

The Casino (meaning small house) was built in the 1760s. It probably had very little function and was certainly very expensive to create, but it is a unique creation of Neoclassical architectural skill, based on the design of a Greek temple.

The Casino at Marino

Structure

From the outside the Casino appears to be a Greek temple of one storey, but in fact the inside is cleverly constructed to hold sixteen rooms in three stories and a basement. The second storey is cleverly camouflaged behind the large door, which only half opens. The windows are made of curved glass and are designed to reflect the exterior and hide the internal walls which run across them. On the roof, the Grecian funerary urns function as chimneys and the columns are hollow to allow rain to run down and collect in tanks as a water supply for the house.

Layout

The plan of the Casino is in the shape of a Greek cross, which stands on a podium. It is only 50 square feet.

Exterior

The exterior is cross-shaped and two Doric columns frame each of the projecting sides.

A rectangular attic storry surmounts the north and south sides, and triangular pediments adorn the east and west sides. Simon Vierpyl was responsible for the carvings on the exterior which is heavily decorated.

Plan of the Casino at Marino

The entablature supported by the columns has relief sculptures of ox sculls and concentric circles, and standing on this are four statues of Bacchus, Ceres, Venus and Apollo that symbolise the love of good living.

The funerary urns on the parapet are the work of James Gandon, who was at that time assistant to Simon Vierpyl. He later made his own mark in Dublin and used the design of the urns again on the Custom House. Large Egyptian-style lions guard the four corners of the stepped podium at ground level.

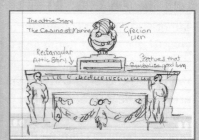

Grecian urn in the attic storey

Interior

The interiors spaces are masterpieces of design. The rooms are all extremely small but they are so well proportioned that there is no sense of crowding. The ceilings are beautifully ornate, with plasterwork by Giovanni Battista Cipriani. Magnificent parquet floors, using exotic woods patterned and geometric in design, cover the hall and main reception room, which faces towards the sea.

The work of a named stuccodore

Relief wall decoration known as stucco (after the Italian word meaning 'plaster') was very popular in fine houses during the eighteenth century in both England and Ireland. The Palladian style, which used motifs inspired by Greek and Roman decoration, dominated the early part of the century.

Francini brothers

The Francini brothers are the most famous stuccodores from the Palladian Period. They were brought over from Italy in 1738 and created stucco in many of Ireland's finest country houses. Most of their work was done in plain white in the Rococo manner, a style associated with swirling ornament with high-relief figures, flowers and garlands. They also introduced the human figure into plasterwork.

Neoclassicism

Michael Stapleton was a Neoclassical Irish master stuccodore. He became prominent in the later part of the eighteenth century. He worked mainly with moulds, and delicate medallions encircled by lace-like patterns are a feature of his work.

Coloured stucco

Examples of Michael Stapleton's work can be found in Lucan House, Trinity College Chapel and Belvedere House. Neoclassical stucco work is seen at its best when it is picked up in colour, and Belvedere House shows Stapleton's work at its finest. The mixture of colours and variety of patterns is a perfect example of the wealth, gaiety, vitality and taste of the Georgian Period. In one of the rooms the ceiling is blue, and the centrepieces and lacework are picked out in white. In another, yellow walls have pale green panels and figures are done in white, while the frieze is done in a russet colour.

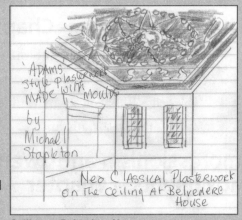

Ceiling at Belvedere House

The lacy effect creates a very grand appearance; this was important at a time when elaborate design and decoration of a house helped to define its owner's social status. In fact, this time of exquisite architecture and plasterwork is often referred to as the 'Irish Renaissance'.

SECTION 2

European Art

Medieval Europe – Chapter 5

- Romanesque and Gothic Architecture and Art
- The International Style
- Fourteenth-Century Painting in Italy

The Renaissance – Chapter 6

- The Early Renaissance in Florence
- The High Renaissance in Florence and Rome
- The High Renaissance in Venice
- The Northern Renaissance

Impressionism and Twentieth-Century Art Movements – Chapter 7

- Impressionism
- Neo-Impressionism
- Post-Impressionism
- Fauvism
- Cubism

Romanesque art and architecture: Eleventh and twelfth centuries

- Gain a clear understanding of the historical background of Medieval Europe
- Fully appreciate the power of the Church and its influence on the art and architecture of the period
- Know the technical changes in architecture
- Appreciate the role of art as a narrative medium and a ready source of instruction for the illiterate population
- Become familiar with examples

Romanesque art was the first international style in Europe since ancient times. It developed sometime after the year AD 1000 and lasted throughout the twelfth century. This was a period of relative peace and prosperity that followed several centuries of war and poverty after the collapse of the Roman Empire.

There was a deep belief in the afterlife throughout all levels of society in Medieval Europe. In a time of great individual faith and piety, prayer and religious practice dominated every aspect of daily life from the cradle to the grave.

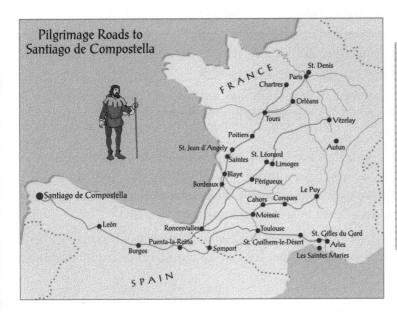

Pilgrimage Roads to Santiago de Compostella

FRANCE

St. Denis
Paris
Chartres
Orléans
Tours
Vézelay
Poitiers
St. Jean d'Angely
Saintes
St. Léonard
Limoges
Autun
Blaye
Bordeaux
Périgueux
Le Puy
Cahors Conques
Santiago de Compostella
Moissac
León
Roncesvalles
Toulouse
St. Gilles du Gard
Puenta-la-Reina
Somport
St. Guilhem-le-Désert
Arles
Burgos
Les Saintes Maries

SPAIN

Pilgrimage routes throughout France

The new millennium had an effect on Medieval European society. There was a widespread fear that the world would end in the year AD 1000 and this led to a great deal of pessimism about the future during the late 900s.

'Romanesque' means 'Roman-like' and refers to the rounded Roman arch, which was the basis for structures built at the time. The term was first used in the early nineteenth century by a French art expert and has been used to describe the style ever after. The style originated in France but it spread quickly as travel in the form of pilgrimages and crusades took the ideas to other parts.

The Church

As prosperity increased there was a renewed interest in learning, philosophy and technology, but the Christian Church remained the dominant influence. The Church had developed during the early Middle Ages and by now it was a powerful, well-organised and wealthy institution.

Monastic orders in particular grew stronger and more influential, but there was intense religious faith in all levels of society. Rich and poor alike undertook long pilgrimages (journeys to sacred places), prayed to the saints, and had deep devotion to relics.

Building of churches

The popularity of pilgrimages had led to a dramatic increase in church building. New stone churches were built along the four main pilgrimage routes. Cluny Abbey (now destroyed) was rebuilt in the Romanesque style. It was the largest and grandest church in the Christian world at the time. Churches on the pilgrimage routes followed this design.

Architecture

- Romanesque churches were based on the model of the Basilica, which was a Roman public building that was mostly used for legal and business matters.
- Like the basilica, the new churches were long rectangular buildings with a central nave and an aisle on either side, separated by an arcade of pillars and arches. At the end of the nave behind the altar area was a small recess called an apse.
- Romanesque builders, however, added transepts to the basic shape. These crossed the nave to form arms on either side, making it a cruciform shape. This allowed pilgrims to walk around the church to view the relics.
- Fire had been a huge problem in older buildings, and wooden roofs had been the cause of many disasters. It was therefore very important that the new churches should have stone roofs.
- Romanesque builders looked to the Roman arch as a model for the vaulting of stone roofs. However, the stone was very heavy and this put great pressure on the vaulting. Supporting walls also had to be very thick, which allowed relatively little space for windows and made the interiors quite dark and gloomy.
- Builders continued to experiment with vaulting and as church architecture developed, towers, smaller chapels, upper level walkways and other features were also added.

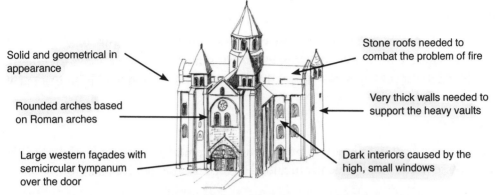

Solid and geometrical in appearance

Rounded arches based on Roman arches

Large western façades with semicircular tympanum over the door

Stone roofs needed to combat the problem of fire

Very thick walls needed to support the heavy vaults

Dark interiors caused by the high, small windows

Characteristics of Romanesque architecture

Romanesque barrel vault

Romanesque groin vault

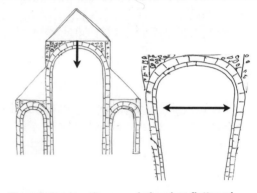

Romanesque arch – rounded arches flattened under pressure and caused the walls to push outward

key point

The heavy stones pushed down on the barrel vaulting that supported the roof, causing the arches to flatten and the walls to buckle outward. This pressure is known as outward thrust. Groin vaulting was developed to counteract the problem, but outward thrust remained a problem for builders of Romanesque churches.

A ring of smaller chapels called radiating chapels (*rayonnant* in French) extending out from the ambulatory

The ambulatory allowed space for pilgrims to walk around and see the relics without disturbing religious services

Cruciform-shaped ground plan based on the roman basilica shape with crosswise transepts

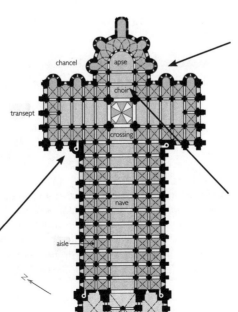

chancel
apse
choir
transept
crossing
nave
aisle

Plan of St Sernin, Toulouse

Sculpture

The most important art form of the period was architectural sculpture on churches. The two spaces for sculpture were the tympanum, the semicircular space above the entrance, and the capital at the top of the supporting columns. This would have been painted at the time.

Capitols

Capitals often featured narrative imagery like an episode from the Bible or the life of a saint. These scenes also frequently included stylised and decorative plant forms.

The Tympanum

Scenes of the Last Judgement were very common. It showed God as the judge and angels welcoming souls to heaven on one side. the other side showed devils and the everlasting torment of hell.

> **key point**
>
> Medieval architectural sculptures like the Last Judgement at St Foy are sometimes referred to as 'sermons in stone'.

Purpose of the sculpture

The purpose of the imagery in the sculpture was to educate people in their faith. Some scenes were intended to frighten visiting pilgrims and remind them to repent of their sins.

Style

The sculpture was carved in relief and there was no attempt at realism.

The human figure

Figures were stylised and non-natural. They tended to be either small and squat or tall and elongated. The drapery (clothing) was treated in a very decorative manner with swirling patterns.

Some of the figures on the capitols were monster-like creatures that were part human and part animal. Many had grotesque facial features and expressions.

> **exam focus**
>
> Exam questions are unlikely to focus on Romanesque architecture alone. It is more common to be asked about the relationship between Romanesque architecture and sculpture, or for a comparison of Romanesque and Gothic styles.

> **exam focus**
>
> It is not enough to be familiar with just one example of Romanesque sculpture. The exam question may ask you to discuss several examples, so study each of the following: tympanum and capitals in Autun; tympanum and capitals in Vézelay; and tympanum in St Foy.

St Foy de Conques

St Foy de Conques is a typical Romanesque pilgrimage church. It was a popular stopping point for pilgrims on the way to Santiago de Compostela. The church houses the relic of St Foy, a young woman martyred for her faith.

A large dome over the crossing was added later to allow more light

Thick walls support a high stone barrel-vaulted roof

Small windows make the interior quite dark

Western façade is large, simple and geometric in design. Creates an impression of massive solidity and strength.

St Foy de Conques

Sculpture

The Last Judgement relief sculpture is on the tympanum over the main door of St Foy de Conques.

Some of the originally coloured paint on sheltered spots

Christ in the centre raises his hand in blessing

An inscription in Latin translates as: 'O sinners, if you do not mend your ways, know that you will suffer a dreadful fate'

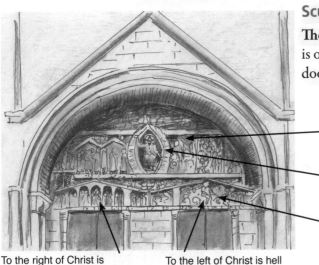

To the right of Christ is heaven, with realistic figures of the apostles and saints

To the left of Christ is hell and the torment of sinners

St Magdalene, Vézelay

This is the largest Romanesque church in France. It was a Benedictine abbey overseen by Cluny and it housed a relic of Mary Magdalene. It was officially listed by Cluny as a major stopping point on the route to Santiago de Compostela. The church was rebuilt around AD 1150, after a devastating fire that killed 1,200 pilgrims. The exterior was badly damaged during the French Revolution but the original interior is very well preserved.

Sculpture

The scene depicts the Pentecost or descent of the Holy Spirit upon the apostles 50 days after the resurrection of Christ.

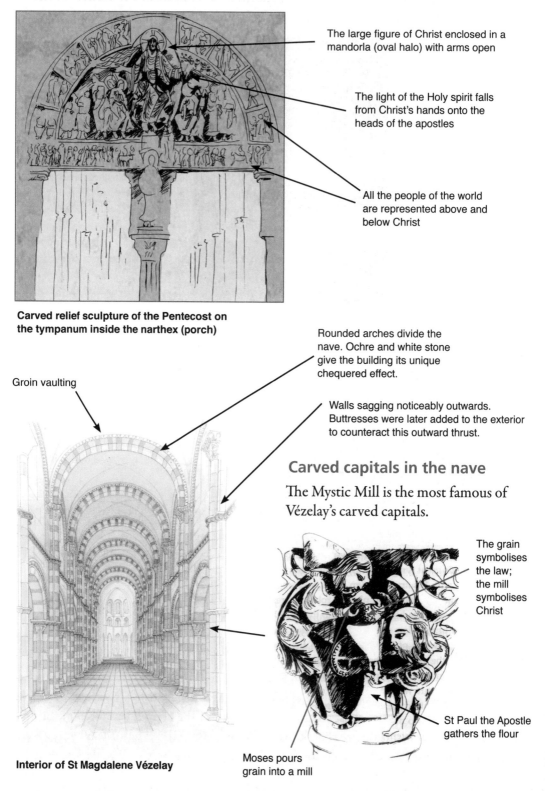

The large figure of Christ enclosed in a mandorla (oval halo) with arms open

The light of the Holy spirit falls from Christ's hands onto the heads of the apostles

All the people of the world are represented above and below Christ

Carved relief sculpture of the Pentecost on the tympanum inside the narthex (porch)

Rounded arches divide the nave. Ochre and white stone give the building its unique chequered effect.

Groin vaulting

Walls sagging noticeably outwards. Buttresses were later added to the exterior to counteract this outward thrust.

Carved capitals in the nave

The Mystic Mill is the most famous of Vézelay's carved capitals.

The grain symbolises the law; the mill symbolises Christ

St Paul the Apostle gathers the flour

Interior of St Magdalene Vézelay

Moses pours grain into a mill

St Lazare, Autun

St Lazare is one of the most important Romanesque churches in France. It was built in the mid-twelfth century. Some later Gothic additions were needed, but the core of the church remains Romanesque. It is famous for its wonderful sculptures by Gislebertus.

The Last Judgement

This is a relief sculpture on the tympanum over the main door on Autun's west façade.

The apostles on Christ's right

St Peter with the large key to heaven

Christ sits impassively inside a great mandorla held by angels

Souls are poured down to hell, where hideous devils torment them

The blessed rejoice and are welcomed to heaven

Souls arise from their coffins and an angel with a flaming sword separates the saved from the damned

The damned are sent naked and trembling to hell. A pair of giant hands pulls up a miserable soul.

The Weighing of Souls

This very famous scene represents the struggle between good and evil.

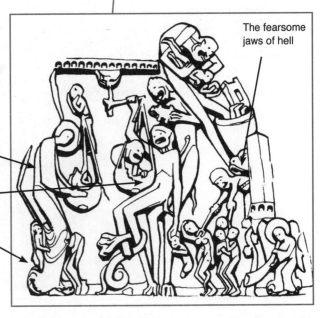

The fearsome jaws of hell

Archangel Michael leans on the scales to help souls go in the right direction

A devil sits in the scales and another pulls on it to make it heavier

Terrified souls cling to archangel Michael's skirts

key point

The simplicity of the storytelling sculpture at Autun tends to appeal to the modern viewer not just because of its intensity but because its expressive, elongated figures have a distinctly abstract quality.

key point

The tympanum at Autun was plastered over in the mid-eighteenth century because the Church had grown embarrassed by its harsh imagery. The head of Christ was sticking out so it was hacked off. The plaster was removed in 1837 and Christ's head was found in a local museum in 1948. Because the tympanum was plastered over it survived the Revolution, while many other artworks were lost.

Carved capitals in the nave

Gislebertus' skills as a sculptor and storyteller can be seen in the narrative scenes on the top of the columns in the nave. **The suicide of Judas** is the most famous of these.

A beautiful ornamental tree contrasts with the horror of the event

Judas hangs himself after betraying Jesus while devils pull on the rope

The scene fits neatly into the shape of the capital in a triangular composition

The dream of the Magi

The angel comes to warn the three kings not to return to Herod but to follow the star. This message is shown very clearly in the scene with the minimum of detail.

The angel points with one hand to the star of Bethlehem, and gently touches one of the sleeping kings with the other

The king wakes and opens one eye

The composition includes ornamental foliage that fits with the awkward shape of the capital

The three kings sleep under a magnificent bedcover, and are clearly identified by their crowns

- Visit www.sacred-destinations.com, following the links for Cluny, Autun, Vézelay and Conques. You will find excellent illustrations and descriptions of important sites of church architecture and sculpture.
- Visit www.wga.hu. Use the search facility to find Gislebertus and you'll see wonderfully detailed images of the tympanum at Autun. You should also search for Vézelay.

For useful resources, go to www.khanacademy.org and search for:

- 'Pentecost and Mission to the Apostles Tympanum'
- 'Last Judgement Tympanum, Cathedral of St Lazare, Autun'
- 'Birth of the Gothic: Abbot Suger and the Ambulatory at St Denis'
- 'Chartres Cathedral'

2016 Ordinary Level paper: Section II, Question 8

The 'Last Judgement' by Gislebertus is illustrated on the accompanying sheet.

Answer (a) and (b).

(a) Describe and discuss the illustration under the following headings:

- Subject matter
- Composition
- Function

(b) Briefly describe and discuss the main features of a Romanesque church or cathedral.

Illustrate your answer.

Marking scheme

Q. 8		Marks
A	Description and discussion of the illustration under headings	30
B	Description and discussion of the main features of a Romanesque church	15
C	Sketches	5
	Total	50

2017 Higher Level paper: Section II, Question 8

'The scenes of judgement and damnation found in Romanesque sculpture contrast greatly with the more serene imagery used in Gothic sculpture.'

Discuss this statement with reference to one named example of Romanesque sculpture and one named example of Gothic sculpture. In your answer refer to subject matter, composition, style and treatment of the human figure.

and

Briefly describe and discuss the main features of Gothic architecture.

Illustrate your answer.

2016 Higher Level paper: Section II, Question 8

'The artistic imagination and skills of Romanesque sculptors allowed images of life, death, judgement and the afterlife to be central to the churches and cathedrals of the time.'

Discuss this statement with reference to a named Romanesque church or cathedral you have studied.

and

Briefly describe and discuss the main architectural features of Romanesque architecture.

Illustrate your answer.

Marking scheme

Q. 8		Marks
A	Named Romanesque church or cathedral	5
B	Discussion of statement with reference to the chosen church or cathedral	20
C	Brief description and discussion of the main architectural features of Romanesque architecture	15
D	Sketches	10
	Total	**50**

SAMPLE EXAM QUESTION

Answer (a), (b), and (c).

(a) Choose and name a work that fits into the following category:

A sculpture by Gislebertus (b. twelfth century)

(b) Discuss the work you have chosen in detail, making reference to the artist, style, composition/design, materials, technique and the period in which it was produced.

(c) Name, and briefly describe and discuss, one other work by the artist you have chosen.

Illustrate your answer.

Marking scheme

Q.		Marks	Notes
A	Discussion on the development of your chosen style of art	10	
B	Discussion on the main characteristics of your chosen style	10	
C	Description and discussion of one named work by a named artist whose work is typical of this style	20	5 for named artist 5 for named work 10 for description
D	Sketches	10	
	Total	50	

SAMPLE ANSWER

In the Romanesque Period, during the eleventh and twelfth century, the Church was the most powerful institution, and Church leaders encouraged people to make pilgrimages to Santiago de Compostela in northern Spain. Building was booming as roads, bridges and particularly churches were built to serve the needs of the thousands of pilgrims on the move throughout Europe.

Romanesque

The word 'Romanesque' means 'Roman-like' and these churches were designed like older Roman basilicas. Church building reached great heights in France, where five new churches were built on each of four main pilgrimage routes. One of these was at Autun in the Burgundy region.

The Last Judgement scene at Autun

A large carved scene on the great semicircular tympanum over the main doorway at Autun depicts the Last Judgement. Such a scene would not have been unusual, but the grotesque imagery here is particularly dramatic and realistic. In scenes like this the most important figures were always the largest, and the huge figure of a judgemental God occupies the central position, while underneath the souls rise from their tombs as angels sound the last trumpet. To the right of God, Peter welcomes the saved souls to heaven; to the left of God, hideous devils wrestle for the souls of those who are being weighed before the damned are dragged off to hell by grotesque demons.

The sculpture was originally carved from separate blocks of stone that were designed to fit together after mounting. It is carved in high relief and some of the figures are almost freestanding but some are distorted to fit the shape. The scene would have been fully coloured in its day.

It was most probably sculpted to scare pilgrims to change their ways, lest they be destined for hell. Facial expressions and gestures were exaggerated for full effect. In an extremely rare occurrence in Medieval art, the inscription 'Gislebertus Hoc Fecit' ('Gislebertus made this') appears on the sculpture beneath the feet of Christ, suggesting that this is the signature of an artist named Gislebertus.

The tympanum at Autun Cathedral

Gislebertus

Gislebertus has an abstract, figurative style. We can see this by his elongated, non-naturalistic figures on the tympanum. The impassive Archangel Michael weighs the souls, while terrified figures hide beneath his robes. An evil-looking devil with long hairy legs and hooves tries to pull down the scale, while another sits in it to make it heavier before a laughing demon pours those condemned forever down a chute towards the gaping jaws of hell and the fires below.

Although this part of the tympanum is quite grotesque overall, Gislebertus also tries to inspire hope and comfort to pilgrims. Along the lintel below the feet of Christ, giant hands grip a tormented soul and various forms of sin are depicted. We see the miser with his heavy money bags, and the adulteress being gnawed by snakes. However, there are also pilgrims on their way to heaven gazing upwards. Symbols on the satchels help us to identify two figures

The Weighing of Souls

The angel with children

as pilgrims. The cross symbolises a pilgrimage taken to Jerusalem, and the shell of St James symbolises another taken from Santiago de Compostela. There is also an angel guiding three children towards heaven. This image must have greatly comforted those whose children had died. This being said, Gislebertus does not hold back in making the devils and hell scene as horrible as possible. We see that he is very creative and imaginative in his work.

The capitals

The capitals on the supporting piers inside the cathedral were all carved by Gislebertus himself and show fine ornamental foliage and expertly fashioned figures. However, their key element is the story itself and the simplicity of its telling. The main purpose of Medieval art was didactic. Everything that people needed to know about their religion was contained in the sculpture in the churches.

The capitals show Gislebertus' skill as a storyteller, but he keeps his narrative clear and direct. The Flight into Egypt shows Mary and the baby Jesus on a donkey, and another image depicts the three kings asleep with an angel warning them not to return to Herod. These shows that Gislebertus has a gentle side, unlike another capital that depicts one of the most famous but truly gruesome images at Autun, the suicide of Judas.

The suicide of Judas

Judas hangs grotesquely from a beautifully depicted tree, helped by two hideous devils who seem to gloat and laugh. The detailed expressive faces of these figures add to the drama of the scene, which has been composed to fit comfortably into the awkward shape of the capitol. The figures of Judas and the two devils form a balanced triangular composition between the curves of the abstract shapes of the tree.

The suicide of Judas

Gislebertus's work can still be seen just as it was in the twelfth century. The great scene of the Last Judgement on the tympanum survived because in later years the imagery was considered crude and vulgar and the Church plastered it over. This meant it survived the French Revolution when so much other religious imagery was destroyed. The plaster was removed in the nineteenth century, revealing the sculpture in almost perfect condition for us to enjoy today.

Gothic art and architecture: Thirteenth and fourteenth centuries

The beginnings of Gothic architecture

- Gothic architecture began in the mid-twelfth century in the Benedictine Abbey of St Denis near Paris. The abbey had fallen into disrepair and the abbot in charge set about a restoration project.
- Abbot Suger was deeply devout and had a vision of God as divine light. He also had a deep love for art and he worked with his architect to design a new style of architecture.

> **key point**
>
> None of the features of Gothic architecture were new; all had been used already in Romanesque. However, the unique combination of these features in the Gothic style made for a completely new way of building.

- The new style took elements of Romanesque architecture like the cross ribbed vault and the pointed arch, but combined them in a new and much more innovative way. Buttresses and flying buttresses were designed to support walls. These, combined with ribbed vaulting, completely solved the problem of outward thrust. This allowed for much thinner walls and much higher buildings.
- Thinner walls meant more space for windows, and Abbot Suger filled these with stained glass. This coloured or 'divine light' falling from on high helped to create a deeply spiritual atmosphere in the interior. The new style soon spread to the area around Paris known as the Île de France, but before too long Gothic had become popular all over Europe.

The Gothic cathedral

During the thirteenth century, important towns in France like Chartres, Tours, Orléans, Amiens and Reims each had its own soaringly high cathedral. They served two important purposes in the town:

- They were its most important status symbol.
- They helped to educate people on their religion through Bible stories featured in the sculpture and glass.

Gothic architecture

The distinctive features of Gothic architecture are the:

- Pointed arch.
- Ribbed vault.
- Flying buttress.
- Ambulatory with radiating chapels.

Pointed arches

Ribbed vault

Gothic tracery

Rose window

Flying buttress

- Clustered columns supporting ribs spreading in different directions.
- Large *clerestory* (upper level) windows.
- Large, round 'rose' windows.
- Tracery and window moulding.

Contrast with Romanesque architecture

- **Pointed arches** were stronger than the rounded Romanesque arch.
- **Rib vaulting** (crosswise vaulting) was a more effective system of supporting stone roofs.
- **Buttresses** and **flying buttresses** supported the walls and solved the problem of outward thrust.
- **Slender pillars** could now support the vaulting system.
- **Thinner walls** allowed for building of much greater height and elegance than Romanesque.
- **Windows could be bigger and could allow** more light than in Romanesque buildings.
- **Windows were filled with coloured stained glass.**
- **Tracery** was ornamental stonework used to support the glass in the windows. It gave them a light and delicate appearance.

Be aware of the different styles within Gothic!
As Gothic architecture developed, a sequence of styles evolved:

- Early Gothic, twelfth century: West façade of Chartres Cathedral.
- High Gothic, thirteenth century: Chartres Cathedral; Notre Dame Cathedral, Paris.
- Rayonnant Gothic, late thirteenth century: Reims Cathedral; Sainte Chapelle, Paris.
- Late or Flamboyant Gothic, fourteenth century: Rouen Cathedral.

Chartres Cathedral

St Denis was very badly damaged during the French Revolution, so the best example of Gothic architecture today is Chartres Cathedral.

Notre Dame de Chartres (our lady of Chartres) is the best preserved of the major French thirteenth-century cathedrals, and its sculpture as well as most of its original stained glass is still intact.

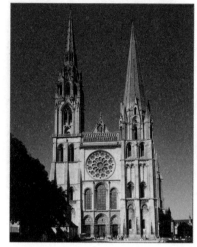

Chartres Cathedral (west façade)

> **key point**
>
> Chartres Cathedral is unique in that it was not destroyed or damaged during the French Revolution. While there have been many restorations over the years, these have not altered its great beauty. It remains today one of the finest examples of thirteenth-century High Gothic architecture, sculpture and glass.

The Relic of the Virgin Mary: Sancta Camisia

The cathedral is dedicated to the Virgin Mary and it was a major pilgrimage site. Its most sacred relic was the *Sancta Camisia*, said to be the gown worn by the Virgin Mary during childbirth.

> **key point**
>
> The word rayonnant in French means deviating and it can describe a development in style. It has nothing at all to do with radiating or 'Rayonnant' chapels found around the choir in most Romanesque and early Gothic churches!

A new cathedral

The old Romanesque cathedral was destroyed by fire in 1194 and it was thought the relic was lost. It was found three days later and it was taken as a sign to build a new and better cathedral.

Structure
Most of the original twelfth century west façade survived the fire; the remainder of the cathedral dates from the thirteenth century. The south spire is the original plain, early-Gothic pyramid dating from the 1140s. Following a lightning strike in 1506, the north tower was replaced with a taller spire in Flamboyant Gothic style.

Flying buttresses
Chartres was one of the first large buldings to make full use of flying buttresses. The large upper windows and three great rose windows (round) over the west door and both transepts allow more light into the interior.

Royal Portal

Chartres west façade sketch

Interior

Slender columns soar dramatically upwards to support the rib vaulting

Large upper stained glass windows intensify the feeling of light and space

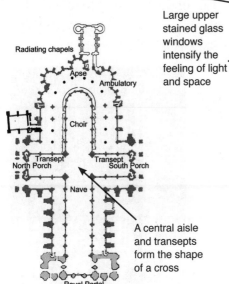

Radiating chapels

Apse

Ambulatory

Choir

Transept North Porch

Transept South Porch

Nave

Royal Portal

A central aisle and transepts form the shape of a cross

The Royal Portal – twelfth century, early Gothic

The theme of the Royal Portal is salvation. In the central tympanum, Christ in Majesty welcomes the visitor.

Three entrance doors are framed on both sides by rows of tall column statues. They are an important part of the overall design of the doorway. They blend with and add to the architecture.

These are some of the most famous sculptures in western art. They show significant development from the Romanesque and have more lifelike facial expressions that are serene and dignified.

The folds in the drapery tend to emphasise their tall, linear quality

Special care has been taken with details like hair, flowing sleeves and girdles. Nobody is quite sure who they represent, but they may be kings and queens of Judea.

Notre Dame Cathedral, Paris

Notre Dame Cathedral was rebuilt in the thirteenth century, when Paris was developing as the main centre of political power and commerce. Part of the cathedral is early Gothic but numerous architects worked on the site. This resulted in several different styles being incorporated before the cathedral was finally completed around 1345.

Reims Cathedral

Built in 1210 after a fire destroyed the original, Reims Cathedral is a later, more developed Gothic style known as 'Rayonnant style'. It was intended that there be seven towers but only two on the western façade were completed and the spires were never built.

Dedicated to the Virgin Mary

Instead of the traditional tympanum, the main doorway at Reims is surmounted by a rose window framed by a triangular sculptured arch. Mary is the central figure in this sculpture.

Rouen Cathedral

Rouen Cathedral is an example of late or Flamboyant Gothic style.

Reims Cathedral

Flamboyant is the name given to a decorative style of late Gothic architecture of the fifteenth century. This can be seen in the highly ornamental tracery on the windows and stonework on the façade that has an almost lacelike appearance.

Gothic sculpture

A change came about during the twelfth century in ordinary people's attitude to God. This was because of a softer attitude in Church teaching.

There were several changes from Romanesque. Some of these were:

- In comparison to Romanesque Gothic images of God, the saints were more hopeful and forgiving.

- Christ was portrayed as a saviour rather than God, the judge of mankind.

Rouen Cathedral

Rouen Cathedral is featured in some very famous images by French Impressionist artist Claude Monet. He painted the cathedral in different lights at different times of the day.

- The grotesque and frightening Romanesque imagery had disappeared, and Devotion to the Virgin Mary had become very popular. Her image was very prominent in Gothic sculpture.

The human figure

Facial expressions on tall elongated figures had become much softer and more lifelike.

Sculpture at Chartres

Column statues or jamb figures are some of the most original and unique features of Gothic sculpture. These figures are featured on the three portals at Chartres. They were carved from the same block of stone that formed the columns on the sides or jambs on both sides of the doorways.

key point

Make sure you can discuss the development of Gothic sculpture and be familiar with examples of early and later style. Compare and contrast in your answer!

The north portal: High Gothic, thirteenth century

The north portal is dedicated to the Virgin Mary and features several female saints.

St Modeste

The graceful image of St Modeste is considered one of the most beautiful statues in the cathedral

The south portal: High Gothic, thirteenth century

The south portal is dedicated to Jesus Christ. He stands in the central bar or trumeau of the doorway. His apostles stand as a column of statues on the jambs of both sides.

She turns her head in a gesture of gentle refinement

She holds a book in one hand and raises the other in blessing

Behind his head is his symbol: the cruciform halo

Jesus is represented as a teacher and has a gentle, caring expression

The Teacher

He holds a book in one hand and the other hand is lifted in blessing

key point

The south portal has a Last Judgement scene. It shows the familiar imagery of Michael weighing the souls as devils fight for them. It is a far less graphic representation than those found on earlier Romanesque churches.

key point

Angel Gabriel from the Annunciation is the famous smiling Angel of Reims. This is the emblem for the city.

Gothic sculpture in Germany

As the Gothic style spread from France, many new and magnificent cathedrals were built in the French style during the thirteenth century in neighbouring countries like England, Spain and the German Rhineland.

Artists travelled to other countries, bringing their skills to local artists.

One of these was a talented sculptor known only as the Naumburg master. He is thought to have trained in France, but his most famous work is in St Peter and Paul's Cathedral at Naumburg.

Ekkehard and Uta

The Naumburg master produced 12 exceptionally fine figures representing the founders of the cathedral. The most famous of these are Count Ekkehard and his wife, Uta.

The clothing, faces and hands are all carved with very fine detail

The poses and gestures have a particularly convincing, real human quality. Both figures still retain a good deal of their original bright colouring.

key point

The figure of Uta with her veil and golden crown is said to have influenced Walt Disney in the creation of queens for his films.

Late Gothic sculpture: Fourteenth century

By the fourteenth century much had changed. Towns had developed and people lived more independently of the Church and the feudal Lords. Art was now produced for the private homes and chapels of wealthy people living in the town.

Curved statuettes

Small statuettes in curved poses were very popular. Figures were also much more human, e.g. sculpture in ivory of the Virgin and Child from the Sainte Chapelle, Paris.

Notre-Dame de Paris

This large fourteenth-century statue was placed in
Notre Dame in the nineteenth century to replace
one destroyed during the Revolution.

The figure is curved and
both mother and baby are
quite naturalistic

Claus Sluter, Burgundy

Claus Sluter came from Haarlem in Holland to work in France for the Dukes of
Burgundy. His most famous work was made for the Carthusian Monastery, located just
outside Dijon.

The Well of Moses

This fountain (late fourteenth century) was damaged during the
French Revolution but still shows the excellence of Sluter's work.
The figures are the prophets from the Old Testament.

The crucifixion scene that
was on top of the fountain
was destroyed

All are extremely lifelike
and realistically portrayed

The lower half with
six life-size figures
and weeping angels
remains intact

With a wrinkled brow and
long beard, Moses is
dressed in a long, flowing
garment

Faces and details
of the clothes are
particularly real

Traces of the original
paint on the stone

Gothic stained glass

Stained glass had been used in the Romanesque Period, but the technique developed during the Gothic era and was far more widely used.

It is not known exactly where the technique came from, but the Abbot Suger at St Denis was the first to explore its possibilities. He employed skilled craftsmen from abroad, and believed that the beauty of stained glass would lift men's souls closer to God. Stained glass was also used to tell stories and to help with the instruction of those who couldn't read or write.

exam focus

Make sure you have enough information to answer a full question on stained glass only, e.g. 'Describe and discuss the Blue Virgin of Chartres and discuss one other example of stained glass'.

Stained glass at Chartres Cathedral

The windows of Chartres Cathedral are some of the oldest and most beautiful in Europe. It is one of the most complete collections of Medieval stained glass in the world.

Stories in the glass

- The tall, pointed, long windows around the nave are called *lancet* windows.
- The very large windows at the upper level of the nave are called *clerestory* windows.
- Each window tells a story. Some are relatively easy to 'read', like those of popular, well-known saints. Some are not so clear today because they reflect older Church teachings.

The Blue Virgin window

This is the most famous stained glass window at Chartres. The central part of the window dates from the twelfth century and it survived the fire in 1194. The composition is long and narrow to fit the shape tall lancet window. Mary is portrayed as a queen and her lap forms a throne for her child. She is queen of both heaven and earth.

Rose windows

There are three large 'rose windows' at Chartres, so called because of their shape. The western rose depicts scenes from the Last Judgement.

Fourteenth-century stained glass: Sainte Chapelle, Paris

- King Louis IX had Sainte Chapelle built as his own private chapel and he used it to house his most precious relic – a fragment of the crown of thorns worn by Jesus.
- The king paid a large sum of money to buy these relics in 1239; he wanted Sainte Chapelle to be perfect.
- The interior is full of light and colour from the exquisite stained glass that completely surrounds the walls on three sides.
- The tall, thin lancet windows are coloured in deep reds and blues that blend together to give a purplish hue.
- A rose window was added in the fifteenth century.
- Structural supports have been kept to the bare minimum to accommodate this huge expanse of stained glass.
- The overall effect is one of fragile beauty.
- Sainte Chapelle suffered major damage during the Revolution, but the windows survived.

Interior Upper Chapel, Sainte Chapelle

2017 Ordinary Level paper: Section II, Question 9

A view of the 'Wilton Diptych' (c. 1395–1399) is illustrated on the accompanying sheet.

Answer (a) and (b).

(a) Describe and discuss this work using the following headings:

- Subject matter
- Layout
- Painting techniques and use of colour

(b) Briefly describe and discuss the function of this work and how the work was constructed.

Illustrate your answer.

For useful resources, go to www.khanacademy.org and search for:

- 'Sainte-Chapelle Paris'
- 'Wilton Diptych'
- Go to www.wga.hu and use the list of artists to search for:
- 'Limbourg brothers' (artists for Les Tres Riches Heures du Duc de Berry)

2014 Higher Level paper: Section II, Question 8

Name and discuss the sculpture illustrated on the accompanying sheet [*The Well of Moses*], making reference to the sculptor, theme, composition, style and the period in which it was produced.

and

Name a cathedral from this period and briefly describe and discuss its main architectural features.

Illustrate your answer.

Marking scheme

Q. 8		Marks	Notes
A	Description and discussion of sculpture illustrated referring to the artists name, subject matter, and composition	15	5 for name 10 for description
B	The treatment of the human figure and period in which it was produced	15	
C	Brief discussion of one other named work by this artist	15	5 for name 10 for discussion
D	Sketches	5	
	Total	50	

The *Wilton Diptych*

The *Wilton Diptych* in the National Gallery in London is a lifelike portrait of Richard II with his patron saints. A diptych is two paintings that are hinged together. The small painting is a perfect example of delicacy and refinement. It shows the flowing lines and the delicate and dainty motifs typical of the International style.

Richard kneels in prayer before the Virgin and her child, who leans towards him playfully.

The saints recommend the young king to the Virgin.

Painted books

It was the custom in the Middle Ages to illustrate calendars with the labours of the month. These were attached to prayer books and were called 'Books of Hours'.

Les Très Riches Heures du Duc de Berry

This was one of the most famous painted books. The Duc de Berry was a patron of the arts. It was painted by the Limbourg brothers from the Netherlands who brought new realism to art. Castles and richly dressed couriers are all portrayed in precise detail. Each month has an illustration. From March to December each month is depicted with one of the great castles and the estates surrounding them.

In May the courtiers wear leaves and garlands to go riding

In September the workers on the estate gather the grapes in front of the great chateau of Saumur

Painting in Italy

The Dominican and Franciscan orders were passionate preachers in late Medieval Europe. They preached in the simple language of the people and mingled with them in cities like Florence and Rome.

St Francis and realism in art

The founder of the Franciscan order was St Francis of Assisi. He had promoted realistic art as a means of explaining the scriptures to ordinary people, the vast majority of whom could not read. His influence brought a new awareness of the role of the narrative or story in art.

Cimabue and Giotto

The Florentine artist Cimabue was the first to work in this new way. He had a widespread reputation in his time, but today is better known for his pupil, Giotto.

Giotto di Bondone

Legend has it that Cimabue found the boy on a hillside drawing sheep on a slate and took him back to Florence. He was apprenticed to Cimabue and learned alongside him in his workshop in Florence. Giotto quickly surpassed his master to become the most famous artist of the time. Giotto's style of painting fell out of favour after his death. His discoveries remained neglected and forgotten until the Renaissance artist Masaccio revived the style.

Giotto's innovations

- He created the illusion of real space.
- He portrayed real people set against real backgrounds, almost like a drama on a stage.
- He used correct proportions, foreshortening and light and shade.
- He had an extraordinary ability to convey human emotion through facial expressions and lifelike gestures.
- He improved on traditional fresco techniques. He worked with wet plaster, which bonded with the colour to make it firm and lasting.

Fresco painting

- *Fresco* means 'fresh' in Italian – it is a type of mural painting.
- Giotto was the first painter to change from working with the traditional *a secco* or dry technique to *fresh*, *buon* or wet plaster.
- Wet plaster only gave the artist a short period of time to work, and traditionally a section was completed in a day.

exam focus

A question on Giotto will often ask you to discuss Giotto's development in painting by comparing it to earlier work by Cimabue.

Madonna Enthroned

Madonna Enthroned or *Ognissanti* (all saints) was a particulary popular image and many artists painted similar versions of it.

Significant differences can be seen between the paintings by Cimabue and Giotto

Giotto includes all the traditional symbols

However, he gives the scene real space with depth

The Virgin has a dignified manner but she is also a real woman in a naturalistic pose

Madonna Enthroned, Cimabue

Ognissanti Madonna, Giotto

The Arena Chapel

- Giotto was employed by a wealthy Paduan merchant called Enrico Scrovegni to decorate the small family chapel.
- He undertook the project of decorating the chapel attached to the Scrovegni Palace to make up for the sins of his father. His father had made his money in banking, but lending money for interest was considered the sin of usury at that time.
- Giotto covered the walls of the small chapel with frescoed scenes from the life of Jesus.
- Memorable scenes from the Arena Chapel include: *The Kiss of Judas* and *The Lament for Christ*.

The Kiss of Judas

This tense and dramatic scene is a powerful contrast between good and evil.

Composition

As Judas reaches out to embrace Jesus, his cloak sweeps forward to cover him. This is central to the composition.

The serene and dignified face of Jesus is in stark contrast to the evil and repellent face of Judas

The two figures look intently at each other

The great yellow cloak brings the eye directly to the expression of both figures as they face each other

The Lament for Christ

Angels wring their hands in gestures of deep anguish

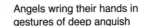

The gestures of the mourners help to lead the eye to the dead Christ

Composition

The diagonal line of the background draws the composition direclty to Mary as she tenderly holds her son's lifeless head

The human figure

The figures are realistic and show very lifelike grieving gestures. They also have real expressions that show deep human emotion.

Dramatic foreshortening make the gestures more real

The mourners have their backs towards us, the viewers, creating an image of a scene set like a drama on a stage

Mary Magdalene holds Jesus' feet and gazes

2016 Ordinary Level paper: Section II, Question 9

'Flight into Egypt' by Giotto (c. 1267–1337) is illustrated on the accompanying sheet.

Answer (a) and (b).

(a) Describe and discuss this work under the following headings:

- Subject matter
- Composition and use of perspective
- Technique and use of colour

(b) Name and briefly describe and discuss one other work by Giotto.

Illustrate your answer.

key point

For useful resources, go to www.khanacademy.org and search for:

- 'Giotto's Arena (Scrovegni) Chapel, Padua' (parts 1, 2, 3 and 4)

Marking scheme

Q. 9		Marks	Notes
A	Description and discussion of the illustration under headings	30	
B	Name, description and discussion of one other work by Giotto	15	5 for name 10 for discussion
C	Sketches	5	
	Total	50	

2017 Higher Level paper: Section II, Question 14

Answer (a), (b), and (c).

(a) Choose and name a work by Giotto (c. 1267/76–1337).

(b) Describe and discuss the work you have chosen in detail, making reference to the artist, subject matter, style, composition, materials, techniques and the period in which the work was produced.

(c) Name and briefly describe and discuss one other work by the artist you have chosen.

Illustrate your answer.

2014 Higher Level paper: Section II, Question 9

'Giotto (c. 1267–1337) created an illusion of depth on a flat surface and portrayed dramatic events as if they were happening on a stage.'

Discuss this statement with reference to a named work by Giotto, commenting on subject matter, composition, style, and the techniques used in his work.

and

Name and briefly discuss one other work by this artist.

Illustrate your answer.

Marking scheme

Q. 9		Marks	Notes
A	Discussion of statement	10	
B	Discussion of named work by Giotto commenting on subject matter, composition, style and the techniques used in his work	15	5 for name 10 for discussion
C	Brief discussion of one other named work by Giotto	15	5 for name 10 for discussion
D	Sketches	10	
	Total	50	

6 The Renaissance

The Renaissance

There are usually **two Renaissance questions** on the paper:

- The first (Question 10) tends to relate to the **Early Renaissance in Florence**: painting, sculpture **or** architecture.
- The second (Question 11) tends to relate to the **High Renaissance**.
- Either question can also relate to the Early Renaissance in Northern Europe, the Renaissance in Germany and England, or the High Renaissance in Venice.

aims

- Appreciate the concept of the 'Renaissance' as applied to the visual arts
- Understand the influences of classical culture and humanism on painting, sculpture and architecture
- Have gained an understanding of the role of patronage in the city-states and the Papacy
- Know and understand the importance of artistic status in Italy
- Appreciate the new status in the representation of the human figure in art
- Understand the changed role of the artist

Rediscovering antiquity

The word *Renaissance* means 'rebirth' in French, and is today mostly associated with the visual arts. It was inspired by the literature, language, culture and art of ancient Greece and Rome. Some of the other reasons for the development of this extraordinary period of creative and intellectual achievement were:

- A new philosophy called **humanism** became widespread among intellectuals. This philosophy valued human achievements because man was God's creation. In humanist philosophy, the ancient worlds of Greece and Rome were considered the highest point of human intellectual achievement. Beauty was regarded as a way of honouring God.

key point

Excellent pictures and information on Renaissance artists can be found on www.wga.hu and www.khanacademy.org (humanities/renaissance-reformation/early-renaissance)

exam focus

To fully answer a question on the Renaissance, you must have a clear understanding of the period during which the art was produced.

Become familiar with artists and artworks from the Early and High Renaissance.

Learn about painting, sculpture and architecture and understand the influence of one on the other.

- Printing helped to spread the new ideas from humanist literature as well as translations from classical works about science and astronomy.
- The growth of European cities contributed greatly to the spread of learning. The main centres of wealth, education and culture were London, Amsterdam, Paris, Vienna, Venice and Florence.

Florence

The Republic of Florence was a small, independent city-state. One of the most powerful and prosperous in Europe, it had a strong woollen industry and its own currency – a gold coin called the florin. This was an important trade coin in Western Europe.

As well as being a thriving commercial centre, the people of Florence had high regard for all things cultural and intellectual. Humanist scholars found it easy to promote the notion of the dignity and importance of humankind in this environment.

The baptistery doors in Florence

The trade guilds

The guilds were major patrons of art in Renaissance Florence. They were:

- associations of master craftsmen that set standards of apprenticeship, qualification and good workmanship.
- extremely powerful politically, and virtually controlled the city's government.
- very wealthy and took financial responsibility for the city's major churches, hospitals and charitable institutions.

> **The construction of Florence Cathedral took over a century. A series of competitions were held at several stages of its completion. These competitions became one of the main driving forces of artistic development in the city.**

Examples of guilds include: the Arte de **Cambrio**, the guild of the bankers; and the Arte dei Mercanti di **Calimala**, the guild of the wool and cloth merchants.

The baptistery

- The cathedral and the baptistery were the responsibility of the Calimala guild.
- The baptistery was dedicated to the patron saint of Florence, St John the Baptist.
- The Calimala restored the building around AD 1200, covering it with green and white marble cladding.
- In the late thirteenth century, they replaced the wooden entrance doors and commissioned the sculptor Andrea Pisano to make new bronze doors.

> Visit www.sacred-destinations.com for a short history of Florence and some detailed pictures of the Baptistery.

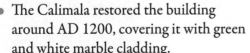

The first baptistery doors: Andrea Pisano

These doors were made of bronze with gilded (thinly layered gold) figures. Twenty-eight relief panels in total show scenes of St John the Baptist's life.

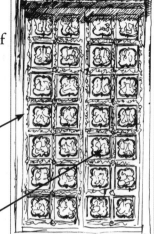

Each of the scenes is enclosed within a quatrefoil shape

His life is featured on the left door

His death is featured on the right door

The competition for the second baptistery doors

The fifteenth century in Florence began with one of the most famous competitions in the history of art. The Calimala celebrated the year 1400 with a competition to design a new set of doors for the baptistery. The brief was to design doors to match the style of Andrea Pisano's for the main doors facing the cathedral. Artists had to submit a trial piece. The strict rules were:

- It had to be a gilded relief sculpture.
- The subject was The Sacrifice of Isaac.
- The details of the story had to be exactly right.
- It had to maintain the same quatrefoil shape as Andrea Pisano's panels.

Seven artists competed but it quickly came down to two intense young rivals: Filippo Brunelleschi (23) and Lorenzo Ghiberti (20). In the end, Ghiberti was awarded the commission. Brunelleschi was bitterly disappointed and left Florence, while Ghiberti worked on the baptistery doors for the rest of his life.

The second baptistery doors: Lorenzo Ghiberti

The subject of the new doors was 'The Life of Christ', and they took Ghiberti 27 years to complete. The new doors also featured 28 panels and the quatrefoil shape. Ghiberti made a great deal of artistic progress over the years, and the scenes are fuller and more adventurous than Pisano's earlier work.

Brunelleschi's technique of perspective influenced Ghiberti

The pose shows classical influence

Baptistry Doors, Lorenzo Ghiberti

The Annunciation

The third baptistery doors: Lorenzo Ghiberti

When the doors were complete, the Calimala immediately agreed a further contract with Ghiberti for a third set. Ghiberti was an architect and master craftsman by now. This meant that he could make decisions on the design of the work himself. The subject matter is the Old Testament. Ghiberti cut the number of panels to ten and introduced an entirely new framing system. It has a more unified appearance and more space for the stories. This new sculptural style was infuenced by Donatello.

East-side baptistery doors

The story of Jacob and Esau panel from the east doors of the baptistery

Several episodes of each story appear in the one panel

Composition

Single-point perspective leads the eye to the central architectural arch and the various groups of figures involved in the story

Subject matter

In the Bible story, Esau, the eldest son, is to receive his father Isaac's blessing, but because he is so hungry after working in the fields all day he allows his younger brother, Jacob, to take his place. Isaac is tricked by his wife Rebecca into conferring this very special honour on his younger son.

The human figure

Ghiberti's studies of the human form can be seen in the figures' naturalistic movements and gestures. The graceful poses of the women in the foreground show classical influence, especially in the soft folds of the drapery. They are three-dimensional and almost free-standing.

key point

Legend has it that Michelangelo called the doors of the baptistery the 'Gates of Paradise' because of their beauty. It is more likely that the name relates to the space between the cathedral and baptistery, which is known as 'Il Paradiso' in Florence because it was once a cemetery.

Art takes priority

- When the doors were finished in 1452 the Calimala made an extraordinary decision. They were so impressed by their splendour that they moved Ghiberti's earlier set to the north door. The new golden doors were now facing the cathedral.
- Placing Old Testament imagery in front of the cathedral was a major change in attitude. For the first time art (not its subject) was more important.

Relief sculpture

During the time of his work on the baptistery doors, Ghiberti came under the influence of other artists like:

- Donatello (one of his former students), who was by now the most prominent sculptor in Florence.
- His old rival Brunelleschi, who had worked out a method of perspective called 'single-point' perspective.

> **key point**
>
> This form of low-relief sculpture was called *rilievo schiacciato* meaning 'squashed' or 'flattened relief'.

Orsanmichele

The Church of Orsanmichele was a former grain store made into a church. All the guilds in Florence were invited to put a statue of its patron saint in niches around the exterior walls of the church.

> **key point**
>
> *Contrapposto* is an Italian word that means 'contrasting poses'. The weight is on one leg and the other is relaxed. The figure's hips and shoulders rest at opposite angles and this tilts the body from hip to shoulder, giving a slight s-curve to the entire torso. It was developed by classical Greek sculptors to avoid stiffness.

Donatello (1386–1466)

Donato di Bardi (better known as Donatello) became the most important sculptor in Florence. His work completely changed the approach to sculpture for generations to come.

Classical influence

- Donatello greatly admired classical works of ancient Greece and Rome.
- He used live models for his studies of the human figure.
- He trained in Ghiberti's studio but worked closely with Filippo Brunelleschi, learning the rules of proportion and perspective.
- He spent some time in Rome with Brunelleschi studying antiquities. This influenced him above all and helped to develop his own unique style of art.

Important works

St George

St George shows strength and courage. His hand on his shield is firm and his gaze is fixed and strong. He is a warrior knight in classical armour.

The tense but determined face is a study of concentrated energy

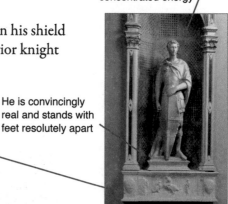

He is convincingly real and stands with feet resolutely apart

St George fighting the dragon on the pedestal. Donatello was the first artist to use single-point perspective in relief sculpture.

St George, Donatello

David

Donatello was also the first artist since classical times to produce a life-sized, fully three-dimensional nude figure.

Material

A rougher bronze finish on the hair and hat

The bronze is highly polished to suggest the texture of the smooth skin

Composition

The s-shape is similar to classical statues but this slim adolescent boy is pure and incorrupt

exam focus

Donatello regularly comes up on exam papers. Have a good understanding of his important role. *St George*, *David* and *Mary Magdalene* are his most famous works, but the *Feast of Herod* is also an important example of his very innovative style.

Mary Magdalene

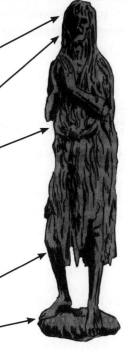

Sad blue eyes stare from hollow sockets, and the half-open mouth shows broken white teeth

Bones protrude from gaunt cheeks

The yellow streaked hair is matted and twisted in tangled curves around the body

Materials

This tragic figure is made from wood which was originally painted in colour

The human figure

The haunting figure represents a timeless image of all human suffering and has a real presence and power to touch the emotions of the viewer. In a gesture of penitence, one knee is slightly bent in a classical contraposto pose.

The long, veined feet still have a suggestion of youthful beauty.

key point

Learn by drawing!
One of the best ways to study these three key works by Donatello is to draw them yourself.

The Feast of Herod

Donatello's first relief in bronze was a scene from the life of John the Baptist on one of six panels on the base of the baptismal font in Siena.

Herod recoils in horror when the severed head arrives before him

Composition

Donatello uses very clever perspective to set several episodes of the story in a complex set of spaces going back through the arches

Subject matter

This highly emotional scene depicts King Herod's birthday feast. He ahs asked the beautiful princess Salome to dance for him. She agrees, but only if he can give her the head of John the Baptist on a platter.

Patronage in fifteenth-century Italy

- The Italian peninsula was a series of independent states ruled by dukes and princes. Milan was one of the largest and most important of these, but Mantua and Urbino had important courts that spent money lavishly on culture and art.

> The primary purpose of religious art was to glorify God but it also enhanced the status of the patron and his family. The patron's taste was reflected in the artist's style.

- Venice, Sienna and Florence were small city-states. Although they were surrounded by enemies, they remained strong and independent.
- Rulers had traditionally been patrons of art, but the new humanist way of thinking gave this even more emphasis. It was important for rulers to be seen to spend generously on fine buildings and works of art.
- Renaissance Florence was a major centre of artistic activities. As well as the guilds, there were many private patrons who commissioned works of art that were mainly religious.

The Medici family

- The family best known for its artistic patronage was the Medici family: Cosimo, his son Piero, and his grandson Lorenzo.
- Cosimo's son Piero died quite young, so his grandson Lorenzo took over the rule of Florence at just 21 years of age. He has become better known as Lorenzo the Magnificent.
- The Medici employed many well-known artists. Amongst the earliest were Fra Angelico and Paulo Ucello.

Main altarpiece of the Chapel at San Marco

- Cosimo de Medici also commissioned Fra Angelico to paint an altarpiece for the high altar in the Church of San Marco, dedicated to Saints Cosmos and Damian.
- When the altarpiece was taken apart later, the nine small pictures in the *predella* (the base) were removed.
- One of these pictures is in the National Gallery Dublin. The scene shows the attempted martyrdom by fire of Saints Cosmos and Damian, along with three of their brothers.
- In the scene, the flames have miraculously spread outwards and have forced the executioners to flee, leaving the saints untouched.
- This small work was carefully planned to create a very clever illusion of space and depth.

Paulo Uccello (1397–1475)

Paulo Uccello was highly regarded in his own time. He became obsessed by mathematical principles in painting. He made three panels for Cosimo de Medici depicting the Battle of San Romano. This was a victory for Florence but was an event of little or no importance. It would have been quickly forgotten but for Uccello's paintings.

The Battle of San Romano Panels

Three panels originally decorated the large hall on the ground floor of the Medici palace but one is now in the Louvre in Paris, one in the Uffizi Gallery in Florence and one is in the National Gallery, London. The panels indicate both the artist's and the patron's fascination with details and weapons of war.

The Battle of San Romano

The painting in London features General Niccolò da Tolentino, who was a mercenary soldier

Style

The painting is completely idealised. General Niccolò da Tolentino wears his ceremonial outfit and sits on his lovely white horse, appearing unaffected by the battle.

Composition

Uccello's preoccupation with single-point perspective and foreshortening can be seen in the shapes, broken lances, posture and proportions of the horse and the fallen soldier in the foreground

The Brancacci Chapel

The Brancacci were one of Florence's rich and powerful banking families. They commissioned a work of art for their private chapel at the side of the Church of St Maria del Carmine. This was to be a source of inspiration for artists for over a century.

The artists

- The family chose a well-established painter called Masolino da Panicale.
- His young assistant Masaccio joined him and they frescoed the panels of the upper walls until Masolino left to work elsewhere.
- Masaccio continued the work on the lower panels until his early death at 27.

key point

Masaccio was the first artist to revive Giotto's innovations of over a hundred years before.

It is important to study Giotto's paintings in order to fully appreciate Masaccio's work.

Masaccio (1401–28)

Masaccio was a remarkable painter who created some of the most monumental works of the early Renaissance. His classical style was restrained, exact, scientific and highly innovative.

The Brancacci Chapel frescoes

The paintings in the Brancacci Chapel are based on episodes from the life of St Peter, but overall represent the story of the salvation.

- Masolino and Masaccio each painted Adam and Eve on the entrance columns of the chapel opposite each other.
- Masolino's *Temptation of Adam* is painted in the elegant courtly style.
- Masaccio's *Expulsion from the Garden of Eden* is much more in early Renaissance style.

Adam and Eve

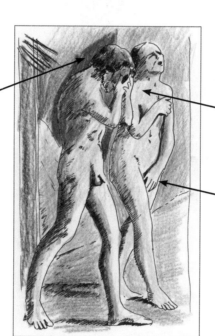

The figures are dramatically expressive as they stumble forward in misery and nakedness. Their sorrow is concentrated in their gestures and faces.

Eve lifts her head to cry out in anguish and Adam covers his face, stumbling forward as he weeps bitter tears of shame and regret

Eve's gesture is similar to a classical statue called *Venus Pudica*, because of how she attempts to cover her nakedness with her hands

In one section of *The Expulsion from the Garden of Eden*, around Adam's head, blue azurite applied to the dry plaster has completely faded and only the grey-blue primer undercolour applied to the wet plaster has remained. The outline is evidence of a giornata or one day's work in fresco.

Masaccio was greatly influenced by Giotto. Like the older artist, Masaccio created real three-dimensional space and realistic solid sculptural figures with naturalistic expressions and gestures. His work caused a sensation in its own time.

The Tribute Money, Brancacci Chapel

This huge scene on the upper level of the chapel relates to the yearly tax payment for the maintenance of the Temple in Jerusalem.

Architectural perspective lines frame the characters and take the eye straight to the face of the central figure of Christ

The tax collector in both episodes are mirror images of each other

The second episode shows Peter crouched at the lakeside

In the third scene, Peter gives the coin to the tax collector at the gate

The central episode focuses on Christ directing Peter to the lake to get a coin from the fish's mouth

Peter's pose is an exact replica of Christ's. This has the effect of locking the main characters of the story into a single unit within the composition. The strong, monumental figures are painted with sculptural-like shadow.

The Trinity

The painting creates the image in perfect perspective of a small chapel with the three persons of the Trinity

The huge figure of God the Father supporting the arms of the cross dominates the scene

All the lines of perspective converge to a single vanishing point at eye level

The Trinity, St Maria Novella, Florence

At the base of the painting below our line of vision is a tomb with a skeleton that tilts forwards

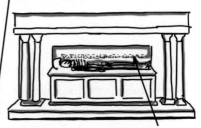

An inscription in Latin reads as an ancient warning. It translates to: 'I was what you are and what I am you shall be.'

The 'Golden Age' of the Renaissance in Florence

Lorenzo the Magnificent

Lorenzo de Medici took over as ruler of Florence at the age of 21, after his father's early death. He was a skilled politician as well as a poet and a generous patron of the arts. Lorenzo's time as ruler became known as the 'Golden Age' of the Florentine Renaissance and he earned the title 'Lorenzo the Magnificent'.

Botticelli (1445–1510)

- The young artist Sandro Botticelli came to live in the Medici Palace when Lorenzo and his brother Giuliano were young. They became friends and shared an interest in humanist literature and philosophy.
- Botticelli's artworks have become the most recognised works of the Florentine Renaissance.
- He trained in the workshop of Fra Filippo Lippi and learned to paint an idealised, slightly melancholic image of feminine beauty.

Mythological themes

- Classical mythology had long been ignored by Christian society because it was considered 'pagan' and morally offensive, but Renaissance humanism greatly changed attitudes towards the subject of ancient gods and goddesses.
- By the mid-fifteenth century, mythology began to reappear in art and literature because it offered all the pagan delights of the naked female body but in a safe, timeless, and heroic world of the imagination.
- The use of allegory made the figures even more acceptable. Lorenzo de Medici, the all-powerful patron in late-fifteenth-century Florence was a humanist and a poet. He introduced Botticelli to classical poetry and his intellectual friends. This encouraged him to explore themes of beauty, love and pleasure in mythology. His most famous paintings, *The Primavera* and *The Birth of Venus*, hung in the Medici Palace for many years.

key point

An allegory is a story, play, poem, picture or other work in which the characters and events can be interpreted to reveal a hidden meaning (typically moral or political).

A linear artist

- Botticelli painted almost entirely with line.
- He used little or no light and shade.
- He also kept his painted surfaces very simple. This can be seen in *The Birth of Venus*, where the waves on the sea are shown with a series of little v's.

Savanarola

- In later life, Botticelli became a follower of the monk Savonarola, who preached against the corrupt lifestyle of the city and the 'paganism' of the Medici.

- In a frenzy of religious intensity, Botticelli began to fear for his salvation.
- He became deeply religious, destroyed some of his earlier paintings and produced only religious works for the rest of his life.
- The artist fell out of favour with his patrons and was all but forgotten until the nineteenth century when his painting became popular again.

Neoplatonism

- Botticelli's *Primavera* is one of the most famous paintings of the Renaissance, but its subject matter was quite controversial and even today is not fully understood.
- It was painted for a member of a humanist group known as the Neoplatonists.
- Neoplatonists greatly admired the Greek philosopher Plato. They believed in a hidden agreement between Christianity and pagan mythology.
- The painting's true meaning may have been suppressed for religious reasons.

Primavera (Allegory of Spring)

All the figures in this painting are from the classical world.

The painting 'reads' from right to left. It begins with Zephyr, the wind, pursuing Chloris, the wood nymph, with flowers falling from her mouth.

All the women are pregnant, symbolising fertility

Venus, the goddess of beauty, celebrates the arrival of spring

Chloris transforms into Flora, scattering blossoms before her

Cupid, the blindfolded son of Venus, shoots his arrow towards the dancing girls

Venus has an expression of melancholy purity like Botticelli's other religious figures

The foliage in the background forms a shape around the figure like a statue of a religious figure set in a niche

The three graces dance in an endless circle of life

The Birth of Venus

This was painted as a wedding present for a member of the Medici family. Botticelli was part of a humanist group in the household who explored classical mythology as a subject for poetry and painting. An ancient figure from mythology was a more acceptable way to paint a female nude figure.

Subject matter

Venus born out at sea and arriving ashore on a shell was a well-known story in classical mythology

The human figure

Venus is elongated with a very long neck and sharply sloping shoulders, but she is the very image of graceful elegance with hair blowing in the wind. She stands in a classical contrapposto pose that echoes the well-known Roman statue of *Venus Pudica*.

Composition

The figure Venus is placed in the very centre of the painting. We focus first on her and the shell before moving to the other figures.

Urbino

Another of Italy's famous centres of art was the little Duchy of Urbino. Its court was famous for its great cultural and artistic activity. This was mainly due to its ruler Duke Federigo da Montefeltro. This former military captain and diplomat set a very high standard of leadership, and Urbino was renowned as a centre of learning.

Piero della Francesca (1415–1492)

Urbino was in a very isolated position in the mountains, so the Duke had to search widely for artists. One of these was Piero della Francesca. Piero was all but forgotten for many years. Today, however, he is regarded as one of the greatest of all Italian painters. He was deeply interested in mathematics and shared many of his patron's intellectual interests. This may be the reason for his austere, intellectual style of painting.

Portraits of the Duke and Duchess of Urbino

Piero painted the famous double portrait of Federigo da Montefeltro and his wife Battista Sforza. The figures are shown in profile in keeping with the new art of portraiture that imitated the medals of ancient Rome.

Battista Sforza of Milan was highly regarded for her intelligence but she died in childbirth

The Duke is also shown from the left because the right side of his face was badly disfigured during a jousting tournament. It was highly unusual to place the couple facing each other in this way. It suggests a sad and never-ending partnership.

The Baptism of Christ

This is one of Piero's early paintings. It was painted for a church in his native town of Sansepolcro.

The Holy Spirit hovers over St John. Gentle coloured light and delicate translucent colours convey a deeply spiritual atmosphere.

Fine lines of gold suggest heavenly light falling on Christ's head

The sky is mirrored in the still water

The figures are solid and strong but are also very graceful, still and serene

Composition
The tree forms a strong vertical line and the leaves curve over with the shape of the arch to create a frame over the figures

Architecture
The Dome of the Cathedral of St Maria del Fiore in Florence

Filippo Brunelleschi left Florence after the competition for the doors of the baptistery. In 1418 he returned, this time to win another equally important competition. This was to design a dome for the Cathedral of St Maria del Fiore. The construction of such a large dome was a problem but Brunelleschi submitted a new and very innovative solution. He also produced a model and he was awarded the commission.

Visit www.sacred-destinations.com to read a short history of the Cathedral of St Maria del Fiore in Florence.

The Dome of St Maria del Fiore, Florence

Filippo Brunelleschi (1377–1446)

Brunelleschi studied art and design, including mechanics. He began in a goldsmith's workshop but went on to become an architect as well as a sculptor, painter and scholar.

He developed the laws of perspective and learned a great deal from the buildings of ancient Rome and his studies of the Pantheon.

The Dome

Brunelleschi's expertise at mathematics and geometry, as well as his knowledge of mechanics, greatly helped his plans for a new dome. His design was unique, technically brilliant and included:

- A self-supporting cupola that had no wooden scaffolding.
- A double shell cupola with a walkway and steps between the walls.

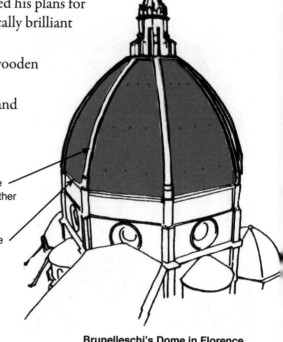

Massive stone ribs held the inner and outer shells together

Stone chains were buried within the masonry, and these strengthened each of the eight faces

Brunelleschi's Dome in Florence

The Lantern

Brunelleschi won another competition to design the lantern on top of the dome but he did not live to see it in place. The lantern has Classical as well as novel architectural features.

Leone Battista Alberti

Leone Battista Alberti was a member of a wealthy banking family that had been exiled from Florence. He spent some time at the Papal Court but then returned to Florence. He was so impressed by all the artistic activity that he wrote a book about it. This was the first Renaissance book about art. Alberti became an architect and, like Brunelleschi, his new classical style became extremely popular in Italy.

The High Renaissance: Rome and Florence

The High Renaissance was a golden age in its own time. Florence was the source of the inspiration but the movement soon spread to Rome. The economy of Rome had been poor but two popes set out to change this. Pope Julius II and later Pope Leo X, son of Lorenzo de Medici, wanted the city returned to its ancient position of cultural and political glory. They employed some of the leading artists and craftsmen of the time. They spent a great deal of money and this resulted in some of the world's most treasured works of art. The rebuilding of St Peter's Basilica began at this time.

Humanism and the High Renaissance

Humanist philosophy greatly influenced the Italian Renaissance. As the period developed, the ideals of classical humanism became even more woven in to both painting and sculpture. Humanists believed in the dignity of man and valued human achievements, but this presented a problem for artists. For centuries, the most important role for artists had been to communicate the Christian message, but if figures looked too real they also ran the risk of looking too human and less spiritual.

High Renaissance artists solved this problem by creating extremely impressive and realistic human figures. They were accurate and naturalistic, but also had a deeply spiritual inner quality. They went beyond merely real to an ideal and divine spiritual beauty.

Draw two works each by Leonardo, Michelangelo and Raphael in detail. Then learn about the artists and the ideals of the High Renaissance.

Innovations in painting

The changes that took place in painting at this time were:

- More realism in figures.
- More lifelike facial features and expressions.
- A greater range of human movement.
- Figures that related to each other in a more natural manner within the compositions.

Remember that Michelangelo was a sculptor, painter and architect!

Craftsman to genius

During the High Renaissance the attitude towards artists changed greatly:

- Leone Battista Alberti and Leonardo da Vinci both wrote books that were very influential in changing the artist's professional and social status.
- Painting was now on a par with other complex intellectual activities.
- Traditionally, artists had been considered mere craftsmen, but now successful artists were expected to be well educated.
- Their opinions were respected and they shared their thoughts with other intellectual, educated people, including their patrons.
- The status of the artist changed radically to the notion of the artist as very special and perhaps even a genius.

High Renaissance artists

- Leonardo da Vinci, Michelangelo and Raphael were regarded as geniuses in their own time.
- This gave them the freedom to pick and choose work.
- Patrons were honoured to have such a high-profile artist work for them.
- They tolerated Leonardo's habit of leaving work unfinished.
- Michelangelo was allowed to argue with the pope.
- Raphael was said to have followers like that of a prince.

Leonardo da Vinci (1452–1519)

Leonardo da Vinci was the oldest and most famous of the great Renaissance masters. He is regarded as the ultimate Renaissance man because of his wide-ranging talents. He had interests from natural science, engineering and architecture to philosophy and art. He designed buildings, drainage systems, weapons of war and a flying machine!

Early life

- Leonardo came from the little town of Vinci in the Tuscan hills.
- He was apprenticed to the painter and sculptor Andrea del Verrocchio in Florence.
- He moved to Milan to work in the court of Ludovico Sforza.

Milan

- The city-state of Milan was wealthy and powerful.
- Its rulers were the Sforza family and they paid for the rebuilding of the Church of Sante Maria delle Grazie.
- It was here that Leonardo painted his famous fresco of the Last Supper.

The Last Supper

Leonardo's version of the Last Supper was very unusual for the time. He used natural gestures and facial expressions to tell the story when Jesus said: 'One of you will betray me', in a silent yet highly dramatic way. The painting is unfortunately in a semi-ruined state. Leonardo was frustrated with the fast-drying fresco. This prevented him from using the kind of fine detail he liked. He therefore experimented and used oil mixed with the tempera paint. This caused problems and within 20 years it began to disintegrate.

Clever perspective suggests that the wall is receding back and all the perspective lines lead to the central figure of Christ

The central figure of Jesus remains serene and dignified

Judas is pushed aside, causing him to be isolated from the group

The apostles are arranged in four groups of three. Some draw away from Christ and others lean towards him.

The apostles reel in horror. Each has an expression of confusion, denial or disbelief.

Scientific interests

- Leonardo recorded his studies of mathematics, geology, the human body and other scientific subjects in his manuscripts.
- He studied anatomy and dissected dead bodies to understand the workings of bones and muscles and the position of the baby in the womb.
- He also made hundreds of drawings of places, people and plants. He made interesting studies of animals, particularly horses.
- He was also interested in atmospheric elements, like rain and dust. He studied their effect on colour.
- He studied perspective and was one the first Italian artists to use atmospheric perspective.

The Virgin of the Rocks

In this painting, the Virgin Mary watches over the infant Christ and John the Baptist in an imaginary enchanted grotto, while a mysterious pointing angel sits with them. There are two versions of this painting: one is in the Louvre in Paris and a later version is in the National Gallery in London.

Strange landscapes of water and rock formations in the background show Leonardo's love of the mysterious

Plants and flowers highlight Leonardo's close studies of nature

Artistic techniques

Leonardo worked with oil paint and used small brushes to achieve very fine detail. Using only a small natural range of colours, he worked slowly and meticulously. He began by covering his canvas in brown tones, and then covered this in layers of very thin paint or glazes. As he worked, he often softened edges and created smooth shadows with his fingers.

Sfumato

He had a huge interest in light and shade and he developed a technique called sfumato (the Italian word for smoke). This softens outlines, allowing a smooth passage from light to shade. It is seen to great effect on faces, both in his religious works and his portraits.

Try an online search of the word 'sfumato' and choose web definitions. The results could be very interesting.

The 'ideal' human figure

As part of his studies of the human figure, Leonardo dissected bodies and studied the physical proportions of men, women and children. He also loved faces and is said to have followed people in the street to study their expressions. Even in his religious paintings, his figures are natural, human and amazingly realistic. He abandoned the traditional halos around the heads of saints, but he created 'ideal' and beautiful human figures that have a deeply spiritual quality.

Portraits

Leonardo painted many portraits of women.

Lady with an Ermine

This is a portrait of Cecilia Gallerani, a prominent lady at the court of Milan. The ermine is a pun on Cecilia's surname.

Instead of a conventional pose, Cecelia is turned to the left. This became the new ideal for elegant female portraiture.

Very elegant line of throat and curved shoulders

The long, tapering fingers are typical of Leonardo's style

Mona Lisa

Leonardo's most famous portrait is *Mona Lisa*. There have been many interpretations of this mysterious painting over the years. The painting is in poor condition because Leonardo experimented with media and this is difficult to restore.

The artist has combined sfumato with chiaroscuro (the balance of light against dark)

Very skillful brushwork and realistic depiction of flesh and clothing

Later life

- Leonardo had to get out of Milan when it was invaded by French troops in 1500.
- He returned to Florence briefly and even went to Rome in the hope of getting commissions from the newly elected Pope Leo X.
- However, the pope was more interested in Raphael Sanzio, a young artist from Urbino, and Leonardo's old rival from Florence, the great Michelangelo Buonarroti.
- Leonardo's work was beginning to be seen as as anti-Christian, so in the end he was forced to leave Italy. He found refuge in the court of the King of France, where he died in 1519.

Michelangelo Buonarroti (1475–1564)

Michelangelo was a painter and an architect, but above everything he was a sculptor. He had keen eye for light and shadow, and understood its role in creating volume and shape both in sculpture and painting.

The human figure

- He became an expert in the portrayal of the human figure.
- He studied anatomy and obtained special permission from the Catholic Church to work with human corpses.
- He also drew from life and made hundreds of sketches. He particularly loved difficult poses, and believed intensely in the beauty of the human body.
- Like Leonardo, his figures are not simply realistic, they are 'idealised' and deeply spiritual.

The position of the artist in society

Michelangelo established the power and independence of the artist in a fundamentally different way from earlier periods. His had his own ideas and expressed them in a intensely personal vision. This was made possible because:

- The status of the artist had been elevated in society.
- There was an open, tolerant, art-loving atmosphere among patrons.

Early life

- Michelangelo spent a short time in the studio of the artist Ghirlandaio as a boy.
- He was first noticed when he was 17 years old. He was by then living in the Palazzo Medici under the protection and financial support of Lorenzo the Magnificent.
- Here he studied from the Medici collection of classical statues.
- He also spent many months copying from Masaccio's frescoes in the Brancacci Chapel.
- After Lorenzo's death, Michelangelo left Florence to find new patrons.
- At 23 years of age, he produced one of his most beautiful works for the tomb of an elderly French cardinal in Rome. This firmly established his name.

Sculpture

The Pietà

The theme of the Pietà was quite common in northern art, but Michelangelo presented the subject in an entirely new manner. The word in religious art always refers to the Virgin grieving over the dead Christ. This was a theme that Michelangelo returned to several times in his life, but the first is probably the most beautiful, elegant and harmonious of all.

Michelangelo's signature on the sash represents the only work he ever signed

Busy diagonal lines normally create vigorous movement in sculpture, but Michelangel's figures remain calm and serene

The figure of Christ is relatively smaller than Mary to bring out the mother and son relationship. The sash across the Virgin's chest emphasises the connection between them.

Composition
The figures are in a triangular shape. To solve the technical problem of laying a grown man on the lap of a seated woman, Michelangelo built up the drapery to form a pyramid of support with the cloth.

Texture
Lines, curves and dark shadows in the Virgin's clothing contrast with the small white marble that conveys an image of lifelessness in Christ's body

Style
The event is presented in the restrained and classical style of Greek sculpture. The figures are idealised, transcending from the mere human to the divine.

The republic as patron

- The young artist returned to Florence in 1500 to undertake a commission for the *Signoria* (governors).
- Florence was a republic again. To celebrate, Michelangelo was asked to make a statue for the cathedral.
- He was given a gigantic block of marble and with it he produced the great statue of *David*.

David

The statue was completed in one year. The Signoria of Florence were so impressed that instead of placing it on the cathedral it was put in the main Piazza of Florence. As the young boy who killed the huge Goliath with one shot from his sling, David symbolises the strength of Florence against its stronger enemies.

Subject
David is depicted in the moment before the battle. His face is fixed in a frown of concentration and his eyes are firmly on the distance. His sling is over his shoulder and he holds the stone in his right hand.

Style
The figure is extremely realistic, but is idealised to a divine level. This perfectly proportioned and flawlessly beautiful male is like a classical statue of an ancient Greek god.

Composition
The figure is tall and narrow because it was carved from a long, rectangular block of marble

4 metres high

A tomb for Pope Julius

- Soon after this, the newly elected Pope Julius II in Rome sent for Michelangelo. He wanted him to work on a very grand tomb. It was to be a huge centrepiece in the new St Peter's in the Vatican.
- Michelangelo began on this immediately, but the tomb of Pope Julius was to be the greatest frustration of his life for the next 40 years.
- He made several starts and changes as the pope kept changing his mind.
- There were to have been about 40 large figures but the only finished figure, *The Dying Slave*, is in the Louvre in Paris.
- Four unfinished slaves are in the Accademia in Florence.

Pope Julius II and St Peter's

- Pope Julius II had a vision of restoring Renaissance Rome to the glory of ancient times.
- He began a huge amount of work on buildings. One of these was a huge new St Peter's Basilica. This meant demolishing the old building that had stood there since the fourth century.

Moses

There were to have been four prophets on Pope Julius's tomb, but Moses was the only one finished.

Frowning and majestic, Moses holds the tablets of stone given to him by God in his huge veined hand. He glares about him with an air of authority.

The strength and energy of this ferocious figure is made all the more intense by the fingers of the left hand, which are twisted through the long strands of his mighty beard

This over-life-sized figure is full of tension and movement. With one leg pulled back he looks as if he could leap up at any second.

Painting

- Michelangelo was upset and angry when Pope Julius decided not to continue with the tomb and to spend the money on the new St Peter's instead.
- The pope asked Michelangelo to paint the ceiling of the largest chapel in the Vatican, the Sistine Chapel.
- Michelangelo protested that he was a sculptor and that painting was an inferior art, but eventually he was persuaded to undertake the project.
- It turned out to be his greatest achievement.
- He painted the ceiling as an illusion of architecture, decorated with sculptural-like figures.
- Michelangelo dismissed his assistants and worked on the fresco entirely alone.
- Working with tremendous dedication and energy, the great artwork took him only four years to complete.

The ceiling of the Sistine Chapel

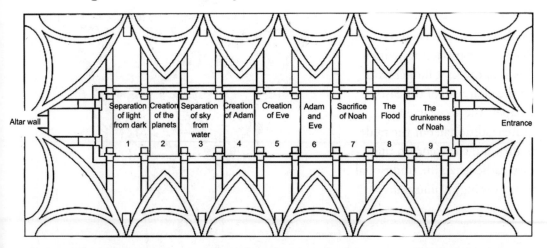

	Separation of light from dark	Creation of the planets	Separation of sky from water	Creation of Adam	Creation of Eve	Adam and Eve	Sacrifice of Noah	The Flood	The drunkeness of Noah	
Altar wall	1	2	3	4	5	6	7	8	9	Entrance

1. The ceiling is divided into three groups that tell the stories of the creation of the world, the creation and fall of man, and the story of Noah

2. All around are the prophets who foretold the coming of Christ and in the corners there are idealised nude youths

3. The panels and shapes are surrounded by painted illusionist architectural forms

The Creation of Adam

God creates surges across the empty sky and reaches out to the reclining figure of Adam. The spark of life is passed from God to man through outstretched fingers that almost touch.

The human figure

Michelangelo's expertise in human anatomy can be seen in the figure of Adam as a perfect young male. The influence of classical sculpture is also evident.

God the Father

Michelangelo created an entirely new imagery for his figures that have come to be accepted to this day. God is portrayed as a stern but athletic figure with a grey long beard and hair.

Composition

Adam fills the lower left corner, enclosed in a diagonal space, while God whirls through the sky in a circular motion formed by the great circle of his billowing cloak filled with angels. The two shapes are connected by the outstretched arms. God's arm is tense; in lifting his arm, Adam mirrors the pose. This is a reminder that man was created in his own image and likeness.

Colours

Traditionally, it had been said that Michelangelo was more suited to sculpture because his colours were so subdued and dull. However, when the ceiling was cleaned in the 1980s, the removal of years of grime revealed Michelangelo's work in brilliant colours. The frescoes were restored to wonderfully vivid lemons, lime greens, pinks and intense blues.

The altar wall:
The Last Judgement

Michelangelo returned to Rome 20 years later to paint a fresco of the Last Judgement on the altar wall of the Sistine Chapel. The scene itself is quite traditional, but the nude figures and the scene on the east, rather than the traditional west, was highly unusual.

Christ in Judgement

With a sweeping movement of the right hand, Christ gestures the damned from his presence and calls the saved towards him

The figure of Christ in the centre of the composition is more of a Greek god than a traditional image

Mary sits by his side but turns her head

St Bartholomew clutches the knife with which he was skinned alive. In the other hand he holds his skin and Michelangelo painted his own portrait there.

Saints who have been martyred for their faith

Michelangelo's architecture

- The architect Donato Bramante began the design of the new St Peter's but the pope asked Michelangelo to take over the project.
- By this time Michelangelo was 81 years old. At first he was reluctant but he later became deeply involved in the project. He disliked Bramante intensely but respected his plans.
- Michelangelo centralised the entire space with a design for a huge dome based on the Dome of Sainta Maria del Fiore in Florence.
- He did not live to see the dome in place. Only the drum (base on which a dome rests) had been completed when he died.
- The dome itself was completed by another architect, but Michelangelo's design is still very impressive.

The Dome of St Peter's

- Corinthian columns in pairs on the drum give the appearance of being part of the stonework but in fact stand away from it like buttresses.
- The whole effect creates a strong vertical upward movement that culminates in the dome above.
- The nave of St Peter's was later lengthened, so in order to fully appreciate Michelangelo's dome, one has to stand well away from the building.

Raphaello Sanzio or Raphael (1483–1520)

- After Leonardo and Michelangelo, the third great name associated with the High Renaissance is Raphael. He did not create an independent or new style, but learned from older artists.
- He absorbed the influence of Leonardo and Michelangelo and made their techniques his own in order to develop his own classical and serene style.
- He grew up in the court of Urbino where his father was a man of culture. He introduced the boy to advanced artistic ideas and humanistic philosophy. This formed the basis of his extraordinary talent.

Influences

Perugino

- Raphael worked as an assistant with the artist Perugino in a large and thriving workshop and it was here that he gained extensive professional knowledge.
- Raphael absorbed Perugino's calm style and the sweet expressions on the faces of the figures in his artworks.
- These expressions became very much part of Raphael's own figures.

Rome

- Raphael made his way to Rome, where he made a deep impression on Pope Julius II.
- He was put in sole charge of painting four large rooms in papal apartments in the Vatican.
- His personality greatly helped his success. He was not as clever as Leonardo nor had he Michelangelo's powerful drive, but he was known for being even-tempered and easy to work with. He completed commissions very quickly without fuss or disagreement.
- Unfortunately Raphael's remarkable career was very short; he died on his 37th birthday.
- He is buried in the Pantheon in Rome.

Madonnas

Raphael is best known for his many images of the Madonna. These were mostly painted during his time in Florence, and Leonardo's influence is very clear.

The Madonna of the Goldfinch

Subject matter

The baby Jesus stretches across his mother's knee to the young St John who offers him a goldfinch. This symbolises Christ's passion and the mother gently helps her son to accept this.

Composition

Michelangelo's influence can be seen in this work by Raphael. The triangular composition is similar to works by Leonardo.

The Madonna della Seggiola (The Madonna of the Chair)

Raphael was working in Rome when Michelangelo was painting the ceiling of the Sistine Chapel. This may have influenced his unusual combination of strong reds, blues, oranges and bright greens.

Composition

A circular shape, or tondo, is difficult to work with because there is no top or bottom. Raphael was a master of composition and has adapted the figures to suit the outline. The figure of Virgin and the child follow the curve.

Jesus' elbow forms the pivotal point of the composition

The School of Athens

Raphael's most celebrated work is in the Vatican in Pope Julius II's rooms or *stanze* in his private residence. The most famous of these is in the Stanza della Segnatura. This was Julius' personal library where important papal documents were signed.

Subject matter

The great fresco celebrates the importance of books and learning, and features ancient Greek figures of geography, mathematics, astronomy and philosophy

Composition

At the centre of the composition, the ancient philosophers Plato and Aristotle stand in an imaginary architectural setting

Portraits

Raphael was also known for his very fine portraits.

Portrait of Leo X

This created a great sensation when it was painted. The portrait is not an idealised image but it does capture his character and suggests the power and splendour of his life.

The richly brocaded cassock and lush velvet cape are depicted with the greatest care. These rich red tones make it one of Raphael's most admired works.

The pope has just glanced up from examination of one of his beautifully illuminated manuscripts

The book and the finely carved bell on the table indicate his interest in the arts

Venice

Venice prospered long after Florence and Rome to become the most splendid city in Italy. Known as the 'Queen of the Adriatic', the city was at the crossroads of East and West, and its commercial fleet dominated Eastern trade with Europe. This powerful independent city-state was the only one to have an overseas empire and it had an exotic mix of cultures. Its unique style of building made it the spectacular city we know today.

Painting in Venice

Colour was the more important element in Venetian painting. Paint was applied directly to the canvas and very loose brushwork resulted in a smooth, velvety texture and a very distinctive style.

Light and colour

With soft light reflecting on the blue lagoons of Venice, sharp edges tend to be blurred and everything is bathed in a soft radiant light. This may have influenced the painters. Light played an important role. It helped them create atmosphere and mystery, particularly in landscape painting.

Painting on canvas

One of the major contributions made by Venice to painting was the development of oil painting on canvas. The damp atmosphere made fresco painting on plastered walls impossible, so artists stretched canvas over wooden frames and primed it with white gesso. This allowed the light to glow through layers of oily paint and glazes.

Artists in Venice

Giorgione da Castlefranco (1478–1510)

- Little is known of Giorgione (meaning 'big Giorgio').
- His dreamlike and mysterious painting brought the new word *poesie* (meaning 'visual poetry') to Renaissance art.
- He died young and his pupil Titian probably finished several of his paintings. Only a few can be definitely attributed to him.
- All of his paintings have a strange, mysterious quality, filled with a hazy light that adds to the moody, romantic atmosphere.

The Tempest

This is one of Giorgione's few surviving works.

A single flash of lightning, just before a storm, makes sharp contrasts in light and shadow

A man stands near the ruins of the architecture, and a mother in the foreground cradles her child under the trees. However, the exact meaning of this atmospheric landscape remains a mystery.

The Sleeping Venus

This is one of the most perfect Renaissance paintings. The goddess of love sleeps in the peace of the countryside, unaware of her nakedness.

The painting is bathed in soft sunlight, creating an atmosphere of poetic beauty

Titian (1485–1576)

- Tiziano Vecellio or Titian became Painter to the Republic of Venice. He was the most expressive painter of his time, and has remained one of the great names in European art.
- He learned his technical skills from Giorgione, and his rich colours and painterly technique are greatly admired.
- Titian left a huge body of work on almost every subject. When he died at about ninety years of age, he was a rich man and the most famous artist in Europe.

Paintings by Titian

Venus of Urbino

Venus of Urbino is similar to Giorgione's silent and untouched landscape, but this would have hung in a private residence and the pose is considerably more erotic. This was a marriage picture and has many symbolic references.

The maids are opening a 'marriage' chest

The little dog curled up on the bed symbolises faithfulness

Ecce Homo

This deeply spiritual painting was painted when Titian was almost 80 years old.

The bright yellow glow of the halo shows this 'man of sorrow' with his face in shadow and downcast eyes

Soft painterly tones make this a deeply moving image of a gentle Christ, bound, tortured, beaten and crowned with thorns

The Early Renaissance in the North

Religious painting

- In the early fifteenth century another important movement in painting was taking place in Flanders.
- This area of northern Europe is Belgium and part of France today but at that time it was all part of the Duchy of Burgundy.
- The cities of Ghent and Bruges were very prosperous and there was a strong demand for religious painting.
- Artists were concerned with realistic space and the human figure, but there was no humanist influence.
- The depiction of naturalism was therefore very different from that seen in Florence.

Flemish painting

- Flemish paintings appear Medieval in style when compared to Italian Renaissance painting. Figures have solemn facial features and awkward figure postures.
- Sacred scenes were often placed in ordinary domestic interiors.
- Perspective was less advanced than in Italy, so space often appeared distorted.
- Despite this, Italian artists were very influenced by northern artists. They greatly admired their careful observation of nature and portrayal of detail in shiny metal, glass, fur and velvet.

Oil painting

- Flemish artists used oil paint. They mixed traditional paint pigment with oil instead of water.
- This was used on wood panels because fresco on walls was not suitable in the damp climate.

- Layers of thin, oily paint had a tinted, translucent look.
- The mixture dried slowly, allowing the artist to blend the colours and make changes more easily.
- The artist had more freedom to depict fine detail.
- The mixture dried to a hard, opaque, enamel-like finish.
- This gave it a smooth, shiny, velvety surface, unlike the quick-drying egg tempera used in Italy that often had a dry and powdery look.

Jan van Eyck (c. 1390–1441)

- Jan van Eyck was one of the main founders of the Flemish school. Van Eyck was painting in Ghent at the same time as Masaccio was working in Florence.
- Van Eyck developed oil painting to a very high level of refinement and skill.
- He also developed 'atmospheric perspective', which means colours and shapes blur in the atmosphere of distant landscape.
- Van Eyck painted microscopic detail with an amazingly high degree of realism.

Madonna of Chancellor Rolin

Subject

Nicholas Rolin was the Chancellor of Burgundy in 1422 and the painting shows him kneeling in silent meditation. He looks up from his prayers to see the Queen of Heaven crowned by an angel and the infant raising his hand in blessing.

Style

Minute details of the room like the tiles on the floor are depicted in perfect perspective. The chancellor's velvet robes and the Virgin's gown are particularly beautifully painted in the finest detail.

Composition

The scene is set inside the chancellor's magnificent palace and the figures are placed opposite each other. They are linked by a series of arches through which a panoramic view can be seen. The town and countryside stretch towards the distant hills in the blurred outlines of atmospheric perspective.

The Arnolfini Portrait

This painting shows the commercial connection between Italy and Burgundy. It features the Italian merchant Giovanni Arnolfini and his fiancée Giovanna Cenami of Bruges. To celebrate their betrothal, the couple wear elaborate ceremonial costumes and hold hands solemnly.

The painting is full of symbolic detail: one candle burning signifies the presence of Christ and the taking of an oath

As a witness at the ceremony, the artist's name appears on the wall above, written in the formal decorative handwriting associated with legal documents. The Latin translates: 'Jan van Eyck was here 1434.'

★ Symbolises death not Marriage ★

The shoes on the floor indicate a holy place for sacred ceremony. The dog represents faithfulness in marriage.

The peculiar stance of the bride suggests pregnancy or may represent the possibility of children in the future

The mirror on the wall is a remarkable piece of miniature painting. The painter and the couple are reflected in reverse.

 key point

The Arnolfini Portrait is one of the best-known paintings in the world and is therefore likely to come up in an exam question from time to time.

 key point

This was the first full-length painting of real people in a real-life event. It gave portraiture a new and more important position.

2017 Ordinary Level paper: Section II, Question 10

The Virgin of the Rocks by Leonardo da Vinci (1452–1519) is illustrated on the accompanying sheet.

Answer (a) and (b).

(a) Describe and discuss this painting using the following headings:

- Subject matter
- Composition and layout
- Light and use of colour

(b) Name and briefly describe and discuss one work by another High Renaissance artist.

Illustrate your answer.

2017 Higher Level paper: Section II, Question 10

'Michelangelo (1475–1564) created awe-inspiring compositions using muscular figures in dramatic poses.'

Discuss this statement with reference to the *Doni Tondo*, illustrated on the accompanying sheet. In your answer refer to subject matter, composition, colour and treatment of the human figure.

and

Briefly describe and discuss one other named work by Michelangelo.

Illustrate your answer.

2015 Higher Level paper: Section II, Question 9

'The "Gates of Paradise" in Florence, illustrated on the accompanying sheet, demonstrates Lorenzo Ghiberti's (c. 1378–1455) great skill as a sculptor.'

Discuss this statement with reference to one named panel from the doors. In your answer refer to subject matter, composition, perspective, and the treatment of the human figure.

and

Briefly describe and discuss one other named sculpture from the Early Renaissance Period.

Illustrate your answer.

key point

For useful resources, go to www.khanacademy.org and search for:

- 'Sculpture and architecture in Florence'
- 'Painting in Florence and Rome'
- More resources can be found at www.italian-renaissance-art.com

Marking scheme

Q. 9		Marks	Notes
A	Discussion of statement	10	
B	Discussion of **one** named panel from 'Gates of Paradise' with reference to subject matter, composition, perspective and the treatment of the human figure	20	5 for name 15 for discussion
C	Name and brief description and discussion of **one** other sculpture from the Early Renaissance Period	15	5 for name 10 for description and discussion
D	Sketches	5	
	Total	**50**	

2015 Higher Level paper: Section II, Question 10

'Leonardo da Vinci's (1452–1519) study of science and nature as well as his acute powers of observation led him to create some of the greatest works of the Renaissance.'

Discuss this statement with reference to the painting [*The Virgin of the Rocks*] illustrated on the accompanying sheet. In your answer refer to the name of the work, subject matter, composition, technique, and the period in which the work was produced.

and

Briefly describe and discuss one other named work by this artist.

Illustrate your answer.

Marking scheme

Q. 10		Marks	Notes
A	Discussion of statement	10	
B	Discussion of painting referring to name, subject matter, composition, technique, and the period in which the work was produced	20	5 for name 15 for discussion
C	Name and brief description and discussion of **one** other work by Leonardo	15	5 for name 10 for description and discussion
D	Sketches	5	
	Total	**50**	

SAMPLE QUESTION (HIGHER LEVEL)

'Masaccio's (1401–1428) grasp of perspective and three-dimensional modelling is seen in *The Tribute Money*, which is illustrated on the accompanying sheet.'

Discuss this statement with detailed reference to *The Tribute Money*, the period in which it was produced, its subject matter, composition, materials and the techniques used in its production.

and

Name and briefly discuss one other artist from this period.

Illustrate your answer.

A colour illustration

When you are given a colour illustration it is very important to look carefully at the work. Refer to it constantly, making it the key element of your essay. Make sure all your points relate to the discussion, e.g. 'Masaccio's (1401–1428) grasp of perspective and three-dimensional modelling'. The choice of another artist is quite open, so any artist you are familiar with from the same period would also be acceptable.

Marking scheme

Q. 9		Marks	Notes
A	Discussion of the statement	10	
B	Discussion of *The Tribute Money* with reference to the period it was produced, its subject matter, composition, materials and the techniques used in its production	20	
C	Name and brief discussion of **one** other artist from this period	15	
D	Sketches	5	
	Total	50	

SAMPLE ANSWER

The Tribute Money is one of a series of frescoes painted by the Renaissance artist Masaccio and another artist named Masolino in the little Brancacci family chapel at the side of the main altar in Santa Maria del Carmine in Florence.

This huge painting shows the full range of the artist's talents and his grasp of perspective. It also shows the influence of contemporary artists Donatello and Brunelleschi, as well as Masaccio's enthusiasm for mathematics and geometry. The figures are solid, sculptural and naturalistic, which shows that Masaccio was drawing from life and his patrons; the Brancacci family were influenced by the philosophy of humanism.

Masaccio

Tomaso Cassai, nicknamed Masaccio, worked in an era of change and innovative thinking. This was associated with the philosophy of humanism that was breathing new life into art. This time of intense artistic activity was later called the 'Renaissance', a French word meaning rebirth. It began in Florence in the early fifteenth century and was inspired by the literature, language, culture and art of classical Rome and Greece.

In this painting we can really see the influence of the artist Giotto, who had broken the tradition of Byzantine painting one hundred years earlier. Masaccio uses the same way of telling an entire story in one painting, which is called a continuous narrative. We can see that he uses the same techniques to depict solid, lifelike figures in a realistic three-dimensional space and, like Giotto, we can see the realistic expressions and gestures the artist used to convey the drama of the story.

Influence of Donatello

Donatello had recently produced some very realistic and lifelike sculpture, and Masaccio's blocky, sculptural figures show the influence of these graceful works. The artist's patrons were also obviously less interested in the ornate splendour of previous painting styles, with their unreal figures and rich gold backgrounds, and, like Masaccio, favoured this newer, simpler, more sculptural style that emphasised humanity in the figures.

Brunelleschi's perspective studies

Early in the fifteenth century, Filippo Brunelleschi had devised a mathematical means to represent space with dramatic reality when he carried out a series of optical experiments. His theory was simple: that the size of an object appears to get smaller the farther away it is from the eye. Brunelleschi worked on his experiments using mirrors and careful calculations, and founded a mathematical system based on a central vanishing point. This meant that all lines leading into the distance came together with the horizon line at a single point in the picture. He passed on this system of linear perspective to his friends in Florence and soon artists like Masaccio began to use the method to create realistic spaces in their paintings.

The Brancacci family

The wealthy Brancacci family gave Masaccio the opportunity to work on a huge scale and use these innovative methods in his monumental work of powerful realism. The affluent bankers had been patrons of a little chapel in the Church of Santa Maria del Carmine in Florence for generations, and they commissioned Masolino and Masaccio to paint a magnificent fresco series based on the life of St Peter. Masolino moved on to another commission and Masaccio continued to work alone in the chapel until he died at the early age of 27.

The Tribute Money is the most dominant scene of the series, and it occupies the upper half of one wall on the left-hand side. The subject matter is based on a small event from the Gospel of St Matthew that tells the story of what happened when Jesus and his disciples were asked to pay a tax to enter the city of Capernaum. This had particular relevance for the Brancacci family because they were bankers and they understood the importance of paying taxes in Florence.

The Tribute Money

A three-part composition

The composition is in three parts, following the traditional manner of featuring several episodes of a story in one painting. The central part shows the tax collector asking Peter for money. Peter refuses but Jesus points to the lake suggesting that it is right to pay what is due. The left part of the painting shows Peter taking money from a fish's mouth at the lakeside, and in the third scene Peter gives the coin to the tax collector at the gate. Masaccio's strong and monumental figures accentuate the smooth roundness of the flesh, and the light on the clothing creates a sculptural-like shadow, adding greatly to the dramatic impact of the story. Peter and Christ both echo each other's pose, standing with one knee bent and one arm outstretched. Both images of the tax collector also mirror each other. The effect of this is to lock the main characters together as a single unit within the composition.

Perspective

Elements of the new art of perspective are clearly seen in this work. Under a beautiful blue sky with white clouds, the picture shows snow-capped mountains fading into the distance, with trees and farmhouses featuring in the middle distance; all are in perfect perspective.

Also, Peter and the tax collector are framed by the crisp architectural outlines of the building on the far right, with the doorway and steps defining the space where the men stand. Even though all the heads of the figures are more or less on one line, their feet tell us how far or near they are in the painting. Jesus is clearly set apart from the group in his pale-coloured robe. If, however, one follows the perspective lines of the roof and steps of the porch they all meet at Jesus' face.

Materials and techniques used

Like Giotto before him and other artists of the time, Masaccio would have used the technique of 'buon' or 'true' fresco for his paintings on the walls of the Brancacci Chapel. This consists of three coats of plaster on a wall. The first two rough coats were allowed to dry and harden before the artist traced the image that he intended to paint onto the wall from a preparatory drawing. The final, smooth coat of plaster was called 'intonaco' and the artist would only apply the exact amount that he could use in one day. This was called a 'giornata' (meaning a full day). The artist always had to be careful with the edges so that each new section of plastering would not stand out from the previous one. He also had to work quickly to paint the area in colour before the plaster dried.

This method was obviously very effective because the paintings in the Brancacci Chapel have been very successfully restored in recent times. The frescoes were badly damaged in a fire in 1771 that darkened the colours, and the work remained like this until the 1980s. Layers of smut were then cleaned away to reveal the powerful images that we see today in all their vibrant colour and detail.

Name and brief discussion of one other artist from this period

Suggestions for Part 2 of the answer:

- Paolo Uccello: The artist's use of perspective could be compared with Masaccio.

- Botticelli: The artist's use of mythology and the nude human figure would make an excellent contrast with Massacio's religious figures and subject matter.

7 Impressionism and Twentieth-Century Art Movements

Impressionism and twentieth-century art movements

The developments in painting in late nineteenth-century France is a very interesting study area, but it is important to fully understand the concepts that the artists had in mind and what they were trying to achieve. Descriptive language is important because the paintings are quite hard to sketch.

aims

- Understand the beginnings of a modern approach to art
- Explore the effect that historical and political events had on art
- Examine how traditions in art were overturned
- Understand the position of art in society
- Become familiar with the Impressionist style, artists and key paintings
- Have an awareness of twentieth-century art movements and how they developed

Art, politics and revolution

Impressionism is one of the most popular of all art movements in Europe. The paintings are colourful, cheerful in mood and easy to understand, but the artists who produced these works were considered dangerous revolutionaries in their own time. Many of the paintings were considered ridiculous and were mocked and jeered after their first exhibition. Art education in France was very rigid, and artists had to follow a very traditional route to become successful. The small group of artists who broke with this system in the mid-nineteenth century became known as the Impressionists. It was many years before their work was accepted and their groundbreaking innovations in painting were fully recognised and admired.

Forerunners of Impressionism

The Academy

- The government of France controlled the *Académie des Beaux-Arts*.
- Students entered the studio of an established artist and studied according to the Academic system.

- The Academy exhibited the work of artists once a year. This exhibition was called the Salon.
- The system did not suit all artists, and in the mid-nineteenth century some searched for other ways to express ideas.

Realism

- Gustave Courbet set out to shock society out of its state of complacency with a new art movement called Realism.
- Realists favoured ordinary scenes of modern life over historical, mythological and religious subjects. They wanted 'truth, not prettiness'.
- *Burial at Ornans*, a painting by Courbet, was exhibited at the 1850–51 Salon. It created an 'explosive reaction' and brought Courbet instant fame.

Barbizon painters

- Artists from the Realist movement worked out of doors (*en plein air*).
- They chose to live outside of Paris in the village of Barbizon, where they sketched directly from nature on the edge of the Forest of Fontainebleau.
- Peasants, houses, the forest and the fields were their sources of inspiration.
- Camille Corot painted out of doors in Normandy, Brittany and around the Forest of Fontainebleau.
- Corot was a transitional figure in painting and was highly influential on younger painters.
- He praised nature and urged his followers to hold fast to the first impression they received from a scene.
- In the end he criticised the Impressionists and condemned their work, but Claude Monet and Pierre Auguste Renoir learned a great deal from him.

Édouard Manet

- The city of Paris was redeveloped during the 1860s.
- In his paintings, Édouard Manet included fashionably-dressed people as an image of a prosperous modern city.
- The public regarded Manet with great suspicion.

Towards Impressionism

- Wealthy industrialists and the new middle class were the art-buying public in the mid-nineteenth century.
- They trusted the 'experts' of the Academy, so their taste in art was rather conservative. Their preference was for story pictures with historical or moral content.
- One of the most popular subjects was classical myths and legends of ancient Greece and Rome.

- Artworks on these subjects were considered serious and respectable. Nude figures were acceptable in this context, but very strict rules applied to the depiction of nude women in artworks generally.
- Female subjects could not look obviously sensual, but were considered perfectly acceptable as nymphs or figures from ancient history.

Jean Auguste Dominique Ingres

- Ingres is associated with Academic art at its most sterile.
- He was a very successful painter and his technique was Academically perfect.
- He believed that paint should be smooth 'as the skin of an onion'.
- To achieve his vision of ideal beauty he often distorted the proportions of his figures.
- He became director of the French Academy and held the position for over 40 years. His ideals developed into a rigid set of formulae.
- Artists who followed his formula were guaranteed success and respectability; those who did not were destined for mediocrity.

The Valpinçon Bather

- This one of the finest works by Ingres. It was criticised originally because of its deliberately distorted proportions in the model's right leg.
- The back view was also considered highly unusual.
- However, the painting cleverly draws the spectator into the tranquil setting, with subtle light.
- The hidden face adds mystery to the scene.

The Valpinçon Bather

La Source

- This painting by Ingres shows a young woman standing at the edge of a rock pool.
- She stretches her arms slowly to empty a water jar over her shoulder. One leg is seductively placed forward in classical pose and she gazes at the viewer with lips apart.
- Despite the seductive pose, the young woman displays a pure, virginal quality.

Influence on artists

- Ingres' work was highly influential on other artists, and the style became very popular.
- *The Birth of Venus* by Alexandre Cabanel was the hit of the 1863 Salon exhibition.

The Birth of Venus

- It was everything that visitors to the Salon sought. The figure is quietly erotic but idealised, passive and without character.
- She is an image of perfection, with masses of luxuriant hair.

Visit www.metmuseum.org for essays on many artists, including Impressionists and Post-Impressionists.

Modernity: Édouard Manet

Édouard Manet was a student of art in the 1850s, when Gustave Courbet's work was causing controversy. He was deeply influenced by the Realist energy, but the provincial paintings were not to the young Manet's taste.

A modern revolution

Manet was born into a prosperous upper-middle-class family and inherited a considerable fortune that made him independently wealthy. He trained in the standard Academic system but it frustrated him. He particularly hated the artificial studio light and affected poses of the models.

Manet said: 'I paint what I see and not what others choose to see.'

A new direction in art

He greatly admired paintings by the old masters but wanted to work in a modern style. He had a clear vision of how to do this by using the grand traditions in a specifically French context. Unfortunately, this vision did not fit with the Academic manner. His drawing line was firm and strong but he rejected long-held Academic values like:

- **The use of an artificial light source from one side.** Instead, Manet chose a direct source like sunlight. This made strong colour contrasts and exaggerated light and darkness.
- **In-between tones of colour in shade to create a smooth rounded finish.** Instead, he used dark colour and strongly contrasting tones that tended to 'flatten out' shadows.
- **Building up colours in thin layers to a very smoothly finished surface.** Instead, he put wet paint on wet and worked quickly using short strokes and even left patches of the canvas unfinished.
- **Painting with imaginary elements.** Instead, he preferred to work directly from reality.
- **Mixing colours carefully.** Instead, he placed colours side by side on the canvas and allowed them to mix in the eye of the viewer.

Manet and the Paris Salon

Manet's work was heavily criticised but he never set out to be a rebel. He had the highest regard for the Paris Salon and wanted more than anything to make his name there. This never changed, even during the 20 years that his submissions were rejected over and over. It greatly upset him but he continued to respect the Salon as an institution.

Manet's paintings

In 1863 the Salon jury rejected an unusually large number of paintings, but Emperor Napoleon III intervened and declared that a separate exhibition of rejected work should be held.

Salon des Refusés

The exhibition was intended to give the public a chance to view the artworks and make up their own minds. The result was the Salon des Refusés (Salon for the Refused). The newspapers wrote about this in mocking terms, and huge numbers of people came just to laugh and jeer at the work that the so-called 'experts' had rejected. Some paintings, however, caused offence and Manet's submission caused particular outrage.

Le Déjeuner sur l'herbe

Manet adapted a well-known Renaissance painting by the Venetian artist Titian, *Concert Champêtre*, for a modern Parisian setting. The artwork caused a great scandal and became one of the most talked-about works at the exhibition.

The picture has several confusing aspects; light in the background comes from above which suggests natural daylight

The light on the figures is directly from the front which suggests studio lighting

The woods are painted quite loosely, but the figures are more finished

Men in everyday modern dress are placed alongside a nude female

Olympia

Manet adapted another Renaissance painting by Titian: *Venus of Urbino*. Olympia was a well-known name for prostitutes in Paris. The jury accepted the painting for the Salon of 1865, but the reaction from the public was one of real hatred. No one appreciated the artist's fine painting methods, splendid colour harmonies and subtle simplification of light and shade.

The critics savaged it. One said: 'The model is puny, the bed covered with cat's footprints, the general effect ugly, but that could be forgiven if it were truthful; even the least beautiful woman has bones, muscles, skin and some sort of colour, whereas on this woman the flesh colour is dirty and the modelling non-existent.'

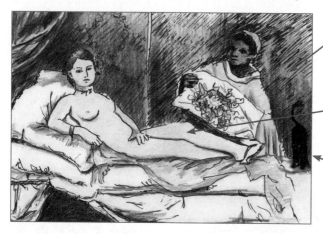

The flat, dark background contrasts with the light skin tones

This modern young woman with a neck-ribbon and bracelet, gazes at the viewer with a cool, confident stare. She is quite unlike the demure classical figure depicted in Titian's painting.

A black cat appears in place of the quietly sleeping dog in Titian's painting; this particularly irritated the critics

Manet's character

Because of his controversial painting, people tended to think that Manet was a rough, revolutionary type. However, this was far from the truth. He was a man of great eloquence and charm who was utterly shattered by the harsh criticisms of his work. He had a cutting wit but his friends all spoke of his goodness and generosity of spirit. Even the critics stressed his 'agreeable character and correct appearance'.

Music in the Tuileries

The gardens of the Tuileries Palace was an attractive place for the fashionable people of Paris to meet and to be seen.

The dark shape of the trees form vertical shapes across the composition. They suggest the black and white keys of the piano.

The influence of photography is seen in figures that are cut in half by the framing edge of the canvas

Manet includes his own self-portrait as well as many of his friends

Association with the Impressionists

Younger painters regarded Manet as the leader of the revolt against the traditions of French art. Claude Monet and other members of the Impressionist group met with him regularly to discuss art in the cafés of Paris and tried to persuade him to join them. He admired and encouraged these artists and was very influenced by their innovations in painting, but he consistently refused to exhibit with the Impressionists.

The Bar at the Folies-Bergère

Manet won recognition for this painting and received a medal of honour. This meant acceptance in the Salon, but it was too late for the artist. By the time he was given the medal he was very ill and had to finish the painting by sitting with his leg up. He died in April 1883, aged 51.

A huge mirror in the background reflects the crowd of people gathered together talking and drinking. Manet has created a strange composition.

Manet persuaded one of the barmaids to pose in his studio. Every detail in the painting has been rendered with meticulous realism.

None of the reflections match and this creates a sense of confusion as the young woman holds firmly to the bar

Impressionism

The Impressionists

- Some of the artists who met Édouard Manet regularly to discuss art became better known as the Impressionists.
- These artists had developed a particular style of painting by working directly from nature out of doors.
- They had tried on several occasions to have their work accepted by the Salon.
- This never came to pass, so in April 1874 they held an independent exhibition.
- The artists included Edgar Degas, Claude Monet, Paul Cézanne, Pierre Auguste Renoir, Camille Pissarro, Alfred Sisley and Berthe Morisot.
- The paintings were mostly simple scenes of landscapes, cityscapes and everyday life.
- They were painted quickly with loose brushstrokes. The artists felt that this captured the life and play of light on the subject better.
- This broke almost every rule of the Academy and visitors to the exhibition were shocked. They could not understand the work and thought it unfinished.
- Critics said that the Impressionists couldn't draw and that their colours were vulgar.

The term 'Impressionism'

- The famous name came about because of a painting in this first exhibition by Claude Monet. It was entitled *Impression: Sunrise*.
- One of the critics made fun of this by calling it an impression of nature and wondering 'who were these "Impressionists"?'
- The group kept the name and had seven more exhibitions.
- They struggled for the next 12 years to gain acceptance. Gradually their popularity grew and they began to have success with the buyers.
- In time, Impressionism became one of the most influential modern movements in art.

Impression: Sunrise

The artist wanted to capture a moment in time as the rapidly changing, shimmering orange light of the morning sun reflected on the water. To create the intense brightness he used contrasting complementary colours. This made the primary colours brighter.

key point

Quick outdoor sketching with loose brushstrokes had always been part of the Academic training. Oil sketches called *esquisses* were very similar to Impressionist paintings, but finished paintings were done in the studio and had very smooth surfaces.

Innovations of Impressionist painting

Impressionist artists:

- Painted directly from nature, out of doors.
- Avoided black and mixed complementary colours to achieve dark tones.
- Examined the effects of bright sunshine or light on water and snow.
- Noticed blue and purple shadows in snow.
- Observed changes in colour on objects in different light.
- Used unmixed primary colours and small strokes to capture the effect of reflected light.
- Used loose brushstrokes to capture movement or quivering light.
- Placed small strokes of colour side by side on the canvas, allowing the colour to blend in the viewer's own vision.

exam focus

Make sure you know!

An exam question in this area may not focus directly on Impressionism or on one of the artists. It is therefore vitally important to know and understand the influences that led up to Impressionism and to study Neo-Impressionism and Post-Impressionism thoroughly.

- Went against the tradition of building up the surface in thin layers or transparent glazes.
- Placed wet paint onto wet paint to create a soft-edged effect.
- Were influenced by photography in the late nineteenth century.
- Were inspired by Japanese prints that had just become available in Paris.

key point

The development of the railway and of portable tin tubes for oil paints made it easier for the nineteenth-century Impressionists to work *en plein air*. Trains allowed them to travel to popular recreation spots, and they could carry materials to these places and paint directly from nature.

Modern subjects

- Impressionist paintings were modern, not just in style, but also in subject matter.
- The Impressionists were influenced by Édouard Manet. Unlike the Barbizon group, who painted rural scenes and peasants, the Impressionists painted modern life in Paris.
- Their paintings featured the suburbs, with fashionably dressed people involved in leisure and entertainment activities.

Claude Monet (1840–1926)

Claude Monet is the most famous Impressionist artist. He was completely dedicated to the idea of painting out of doors and always tried to capture a single moment of time and light in his painting. Throughout his life he worked to achieve this effect, and in the end his paintings became almost abstract, with swirling colours dissolving into light.

Early influences

Monet came from Le Havre in Normandy and he began painting there before going to Paris to study. Here he met Camille Pissarro and the Barbizon painters. Together they worked *en plein air* (out of doors) in the Forest of Fontainbleu near Paris.

Paris

During his studies at Charles Gleyre's studio in Paris he met fellow students Frederic Bazille, Alfred Sisley and Pierre Auguste Renoir, and met with others in the Café Guerbois to have lively discussions on art. The group included other young artists like Paul Cézanne and Edgar Degas.

Financial difficulties

Monet's work was rejected consistently by the Salon and because of this he suffered a good deal financially. In spite of this he spent the summer of 1869 painting riverside pictures with his friend Renoir, and this really marked the beginning of Impressionism.

La Grenouillère

Monet and Renoir painted several scenes like this together at La Grenouillère (the Frog Pond) on the banks of the Seine just outside Paris.

Japonisme
Monet was influenced throughout his career by Japanese woodblock prints that were widely available in Paris at an affordable price.

Long brushstrokes and dabs of colour emphasise the patterns of light on water

Durand Ruel

Monet was introduced to the art dealer Durand-Ruel who had a premises in Paris. He bought a good deal of Monet's work. He was to remain one of the great champions of the Impressionists and it was he who encouraged them to exhibit on their own.

In 1874, Monet and his colleagues organised their first independent exhibition. It created a huge scandal and made no money, but it gave them their famous name after a critic wrote mockingly of Claude Monet's painting *Impression: Sunrise*. The Impressionists went on to have several more exhibitions and each of them eventually achieved success with their work.

Regatta at Argenteuil

Monet lived for a while at Argenteuil, a village on the Seine near Paris. He painted some of his most famous works here, sitting on the river bank.

Style
In this splendid study of reflections, the artist has used slabs of pure colour to suggest the shimmering effect of the reflections of sails and the buildings on the river

Composition
The horizontal lines of the landscape are broken by reflections. The composition is centred by the tall triangular shapes of the white sails.

Success

Life remained hard for Claude Monet for many years, and it was to be the late 1880s before his paintings began to sell properly. By this time his wife Camille had died and he was left with two small children.

Giverny

He later married Alice Hochedé and bought a house in the small village of Giverny. He and Alice lived there with his two sons and her six children. He developed his famous water garden with a Japanese bridge and painted there until the end of his life.

Waterlily Pond: Green Harmony

Although Monet loved plants and flowers, he was not interested in distinguishing them in a painting. He was more interested in the reflections on the water. No sky or horizon breaks the rich carpet of colour, with brushstrokes of yellow, pink and lavender woven in with the shimmering green of the plants. The scene has been compressed into a square that is crossed over by the gentle curve of the bridge.

Travelling in France

During the 1870s and 1880s Monet gradually refined his technique. From 1890 he concentrated on a series of pictures in which he painted the same subject at different times of the day in different lights. *Haystacks* and *Rouen Cathedral* are the best known examples of these.

Haystacks, End of Summer

Rouen Cathedral, Full Sunlight, Harmony in Blue and Gold

In 1914 he had a special studio built in the grounds of his house and here he worked on huge canvases. In the last years of his life, he painted a series of water lilies called *Les Grandes Decorations*. He donated these to the French state and they are now displayed as he intended in two oval-shaped rooms in the Musée d'Orangerie in Paris, bathed in natural light from the glass roof.

Camille Pissarro (1830–1903)

Camille Pissarro was a very important figure in the Impressionist movement. He was about 10 years older than the others and he constantly advised and encouraged them. He organised the exhibitions and was the one who exhibited at all eight Impressionist shows. As well as teaching the younger artists, he also learned from them; and yet he remained insecure about his own his work.

Working with the Impressionists

Throughout his working life, Pissarro:

- painted outdoors in winter and summer
- worked with other artists – especially Monet
- introduced the art dealer Durand Ruel to the other artists
- organised the Impressionist exhibitions
- suffered great financial losses before becoming successful late in life.

Style and techniques

Pissarro's landscapes included river banks or views of winding roadways. Throughout his career he relentlessly searched for the perfect method of expressing himself. One of his favourite subjects was that of houses half-hidden by trees, which created a broken design over the canvas.

Red Roofs, Corner of a Village, Winter

A cluster of houses with red roofs can be seen behind bare winter trees glistening in the winter sunshine

The effect is more impressive because of its rich surface. It is painted with small, thick brushstrokes.

The Church and Farm of Eragny

This is more freely painted than Pisarro's earlier work. It is a beautiful study of warm, diffused sunlight.

Pierre Auguste Renoir (1841–1919)

Pierre Auguste Renoir met Pissarro and Claude Monet at the studio in Paris where they were both students. They painted landscapes out of doors and worked very closely together. Their paintings in the early years were remarkably similar, but Renoir later focused more on the human figure. Renoir liked to paint people enjoying themselves and was often criticised for this but he said: 'Why shouldn't art be pretty? There are enough unpleasant things in the world.'

Like the other Impressionists, he endured hardship early in his career until art dealer Durand-Ruel found regular buyers for his work. In later life he concentrated on nude female figures. The figures have the soft, pearly skin texture for which the artist has become renowned.

Dance at Le Moulin de la Galette

This was painted at the site over one summer entirely *en plein air*. Several friends posed for the artist.

Renoir managed to gather numerous figures together in one composition. Dappled light falling through the leaves unites these groups.

Luncheon of the Boating Party

The scene is set in a restaurant at a favourite spot for boating enthusiasts and their girlfriends. The woman on the left-hand side with the dog is Aline Charigot, Renoir's future wife and favourite model. The space is broken up by colour and shape; it is set out of doors but it has an indoor intimate atmosphere. The eye is drawn around the composition from the still life on the table and the interchange of glances among the figures.

The Umbrellas

Renoir abandoned Impressionism for a while and his style changed after he visited Italy and studied Italian art. *The Umbrellas* was painted over a number of years and the changes in style are obvious.

Composition

The eye is drawn around the painting in a rhythmic pattern of blues and grey and abstract geometric shapes created by the open umbrellas. The cut-off figures shows the influence of photography.

The figures on the right are painted in the Impressionist style, with bright colours and loose brushwork. The two figures on the left are more 'finished' and more subdued in colour.

Edgar Degas (1834–1917)

Edgar Degas took part in most of the Impressionist exhibitions and was one of its most important members. However, his work set him apart in several ways from the other painters. He always hated the term 'Impressionist', and never considered himself as that. He preferred to call himself a 'Realist' or an 'Independent'. He too tried to capture fleeting moments in time, but he intensely disliked outdoor or *plein air* painting.

Techniques and style

Degas was trained in the Academic system and had the greatest of respect for this. He was a wonderful draughtsman and believed in the importance of drawing. He was a great admirer of the old masters and while he drew heavily on these traditions, he preferred to depict modern life in his painting. His work featured contemporary scenes at racecourses, theatres and cafés.

Painting in the studio

He sketched outdoors but always completed the work in his studio where he worked slowly and meticulously in a wide range of media. These including oil, watercolour, chalk, pastel, pencil, etching and photography, and he often experimented with these media together.

Pastel drawings

Degas produced many of his drawings in pastel, especially when his eyesight deteriorated. Often, he dampened the surface of the paper to achieve the effect he wanted.

Japanese prints

Degas became interested in Japanese prints and this led him to experiment with unusual angles. His subjects are often cropped at the edges. He enjoyed the discussions on art in the Café Dubois with Édouard Manet and the other young artists, but he had an aloof manner and sharp tongue and they found him difficult. He had very few close friends and apparently no love affairs. He was intensely private, particularly about his studio.

Café scenes

The café was the meeting place of Parisian society. Both Degas and Manet painted scenes in cafés. However, Degas' scenes could not have been more different to those of Manet.

The Absinthe Drinker

The scene in this Degas painting seems to reflect nineteenth-century public concern about alcoholism and, in particular, the increase in women's drinking.

Composition

The tables are set in a zigzag manner across the painting towards the viewer

Subject

A man and a woman sit at a table in a café. The light in the café suggests it is morning and the woman sits with shoulders slumped, a glass of absinthe in front of her.

The woman's legs are splayed out, her eyes are downcast and she has an expression of hopelessness on her face. The man appears to be drinking cold black coffee, probably to relieve a hangover.

A pen and a newspaper are on the table. Degas has signed his name, creating the effect of placing us at the table where the artist has been sitting to observe the scene.

The Opera

Degas is most famous for his countless images of dancers. He produced a huge number of paintings and pastel drawings on paper over his career. He frequently visited the Paris Opera to sketch performances, but he also focused on the dancers' gestures and poses as they practised, waited and stretched in the rehearsal room. He brought the dancers to his studio, where he had a model spiral staircase that can often be seen in his paintings.

The Dance Class

This is one of Degas' most famous ballet pictures. It was shown at the first Impressionist exhibition of 1874.

Typical Degas gestures: one dancer scratches her back and the other twists her earring as she reads

Composition

Some of gthe dancers wear a red flower in their hair, and these spots of colour link the composition from the dancer in the foreground to others around the room. The dancers and their mothers are placed in a complex arrangement of groups on three sides of the famous teacher Jules Perrot.

A watering can was used to keep the floorboards moist and non-slippery for the dancers

A little dog, standing with one of the girls, probably wandered over from one of the girls' mothers.

The floor stretching in a sharp diagonal line is the most important feature of the composition

Influence of photography

Figures cut off show the influence of the new art of photography. Degas was fascinated by photography.

Horses

Degas drew and painted all kinds of horses, including racehorses and scenes from the racetrack. Horse racing clubs in Paris were based on the British model and were very exclusive. Both Manet and Degas had friends among the upper classes who frequented these clubs. The newly developed racetrack of Le Longchamp was one of the most fashionable sites in Paris.

Racehorses at Longchamp

The horses gather in groups before the race. The diagonal of the horses on the left and the line of trees have the effect of framing the three riders in the foreground.

Alfred Sisley (1839–1899)

Alfred Sisley tends to be overlooked in the history of Impressionism, yet he had a quiet, steady talent. His work is quite dramatic and powerful and his snowscapes in particular have a gentle, almost poetic quality. Like the other Impressionists, he worked in areas outside of Paris along the river Seine at Bougival, Argenteuil and Louveciennes.

Impressionist years

He exhibited in the first Impressionist exhibition of 1874 and in some of the later exhibitions. Although his work can be considered 'pure Impressionism' and Monet's influence was strong, he did not attract the same scornful criticism as the others. Sisley's depictions of the Seine in flood are 'pure' Impressionism. This is a remarkable series of paintings showing villages overrun by floods. Many consider these peaceful images of nature to be his finest work.

Flood at Port Marly

Impressionist exhibitions

- Between 1874 and 1886, the Impressionists had eight exhibitions in Paris and one in New York.
- These exhibitions varied quite a bit.
- The art collector Paul Durand-Ruel supported the artists, but the period after the Franco-Prussian war was a difficult time in which to buy and sell art.
- Ruel's support gave the Impressionists the confidence to mount an independent exhibition.

The Anonymous Society of Artists

- The group chose 'The Anonymous Society of Artists' as the title for their first exhibition.
- The reviews were bad, the exhibition was badly attended and the artists suffered huge financial losses.
- However, the term 'Impressionism' had been established.
- Two years later they came together again but this exhibition was even less well attended. The reviews were no better.
- Edgar Degas was a member of the group, but he was dissatisfied with the name 'Impressionism' as well as with the predominant style of painting.
- Degas argued and disagreed with his colleagues a lot and eventually left the group.
- Over the years there were eight Impressionist exhibitions in Paris and a final one was held in America.

Impressionism in America

- The American artist Mary Cassatt was a substantial contributor to the last exhibition in Paris.
- Her American contacts were vital in helping Durand-Ruel organise a huge exhibition in New York in 1886.
- American buyers brought the long-awaited financial success to the artists.
- By this time, all members of the group had gone their separate ways.

Neo-Impressionism

At the last Impressionist exhibition in 1886, Georges Seurat exhibited a huge painting called *A Sunday Afternoon on the Island of La Grande Jatte.* It was the main attraction of the show and stunned the Parisian art world. Using colour theory in a completely different way, the young artist challenged the accepted Impressionist style. His technique, based on points of pure colour, was known as Neo-Impressionism.

This systematic logical method involved:

- Placing hundreds of small touches of complementary colours together to capture the effect of colour and light in a new and 'scientific' way.

- Optical mixing – the creation of an optical illusion as the colours combined before the spectators' eyes but remained glowing and light.
- The use of these small dots or points of colour gave rise to the name 'Pointillism', and was immediately recognised as a new direction for modern painting. The style, however, was very laborious and did not last very long.

Pointillism

- 'Scientific Impressionism', 'Divisionism' or 'Pointillism' was now attracting the attention of the press.
- The art critic Félix Fénéon was particularly impressed, and his articles created tension between the Neo-Impressionists and Claude Monet's ideas.
- Fénéon first used the term 'Neo-Impressionism' and described it as a 'conscious and scientific' approach towards the problems of colour and light.
- According to Feneon: 'Seurat's divisionist art was superior to Impressionism and the most innovative style of the day.'

Georges Seurat (1859–1891)

After his studies at the École des Beaux Arts, Georges Seurat became deeply interested in scientific theories on colour and vision. He spent two years devoting himself to black and white drawing.

Bathers at Asnières

Subject

This huge canvas depicts people who are probably workers from the nearby factories. They seem to be taking advantage of some leisure time to swim and relax on the riverbank at the popular bathing place of Asnières.

Style

The painting has a vibrant, luminous quality, but the artist had not yet fully developed his Pointillistic technique

Composition

Diagonal lines bring the eye from left to right to focus directly on the pale-skinned youth sitting on the bank and the boy standing in the water

A Sunday Afternoon on the Island of La Grand Jatte

Composition

The figures are carefully placed so that they all can be seen easily. The sharp diagonal line of the water creates an illusion of space. The areas of light and shade on the grass take the eye steadily back into the composition.

Style

The huge painting is spectacularly bright and more formal-looking than Impressionism

Scientific technique:
Divisionism or Pointillism

By separating colour and applying the paint in small strokes or dots (points), the artist made use of the new scientific research. 'Optical mixing' meant that from a distance colours blended together in the spectator's eye.

The statuesque peole are seen only in profile or directly from the front. This gives the work a still, monumental appearance, as well as a timeless and somewhat mysterious quality.

Paul Signac (1863–1935)

- Paul Signac was strongly influenced by Impressionism. He became enthusiastically involved with the small group of artists and the theories of Pointillism or Divisionism.
- He was a keen sailor and his paintings are mainly seascapes from Le Havre to Marseilles, Collioure, St-Tropez and even Venice.
- He had a more outgoing personality than Seurat and his enthusiasm was of immense benefit to him.
- Georges Seurat died at the age of 31. Signac became the leader of the Neo-Impressionists, but without Seurat the movement came to an end.

Post-Impressionism

In the late 1880s, a group of young painters broke away from Impressionism. Each abandoned naturalism in favour of their own highly personal art that expressed emotions rather than simply visual impressions. Some concentrated on themes of deeper symbolism. These artists are today called Post-Impressionists, but for the most part they worked independently and did not view themselves as part of a collective movement.

Make sure you understand the influence of artistic movements like the Impressionists and Post-Impressionists on later artists. Learn to discuss this and make comparisons in your answers.

The Post-Impressionists

The term was first used by the British art critic Roger Fry in 1910 in an exhibition in London. The artists included Paul Cézanne, Paul Gauguin, Vincent van Gogh and Georges Seurat. These artists had a major influence on generations of artists to follow. Their work laid the foundation for some of the major movements of early twentieth century, like Expressionism, Cubism and Fauvism.

Paul Cézanne (1839–1906)

Paul Cézanne was one of the most influential artists in twentieth-century painting. He inspired generations of modern artists but it was many years before his genius was appreciated. He suffered rejection and ridicule, and his achievements in painting were recognised only in the later years of his life, by which time he was an embittered recluse.

Links with Impressionism

Cézanne came to Paris from Aix-en-Provence in the South of France. Here he came in contact with the Impressionists and Pissarro. He exhibited at some of their shows but he was never really an Impressionist and he had a vision in art beyond any of those working around him.

Influence of Pissarro

The real strength in his work appeared when he began to work out of doors with Pissarro at Auvers-sur-Oise, a village in the countryside near Paris, in 1872. Pissarro's emphasis on meticulous observation of nature influenced Cézanne's work in a profound way. He listened to the older artist's advice and it led to a transformation in his painting.

Aix-en-Provence

- Cézanne had always admired the great masters from the past and had constantly struggled to make his painting 'solid and enduring like the art in the museums'.
- He became very critical of the Impressionist artists' obsession with colour and light. He thought this would lead to a collapse of structure and that the paintings would eventually be no more than a brightly coloured, blurred haze.
- Returning to his native town of Aix-en-Provence he sought to achieve his aims by working with nature in the dry, transparent air. After he inherited his father's wealth, Cézanne was free from financial worries and remained in Aix painting right up to the moment of his death in 1906.

Struggles in painting

Cézanne's work is strikingly original, but throughout his career he battled with contradictory forces that caused his painting to be slow and painful. He:

- sought to go beyond the disorderly aspect of Impressionism
- wished to preserve the freshness of nature evident in Impressionist painting.

Subjects

Cézanne painted the landscape around Aix and Marseilles, but he also worked in his studio. For him the subject itself was of little or no importance. He painted nudes, but the flesh did not interest him. He used the bodies only to build up the structure in his painting. He preferred to work with inanimate objects, such as pieces of fruit, because they did not move or talk. Cézanne's innovations included:

- Concentration on the colour and shape
- Pushing forms towards geometric shapes. He famously remarked that painters should 'treat nature as a cylinder, sphere or cone'.
- Placing an emphasis on structure and composition
- The use of multiple viewpoints and distorting objects
- Adjusting the rules of perspective to suit the composition.

Cézanne's working techniques included:

- Building up the structure of the painting slowly with strong blocks of colour
- Carefully using the brush in even horizontal strokes, allowing the objects to interlock
- Avoiding the traditional method of perspective by using horizontal and vertical strokes to create depth.

Madame Cézanne in a Red Armchair

Cézanne painted many portraits of his wife Hortense but they convey very little about her character. She had to sit for hours without moving so the pose was always simple.

Madame Cézanne is dressed in a striped gown and seated on a richly coloured red chair, set against a strongly patterned wallpaper. However, the model's solemn appearance has a quality of inner stillness that makes it very moving.

Still Life with Apples and Oranges

The fruit, in vibrant glowing colour, spills from the plate onto folds of white cloth

The background of loudly patterned cloth is painted with dramatic energy in its deep twists and folds

Composition

The fruit, table and chair are shown from different viewpoints to emphasise the structure and form

Perspective has been adjusted to tilt the table forward in the interests of composition

Montagne Sainte-Victoire with Large Pine

The strong and permanent shape of the solid limestone mountain rising out of the surrounding countryside continued to fascinate Cézanne throughout the later part of his career.

In the early versions, a pine tree is often used to frame the composition

The picture recedes into the distance and Cézanne includes details like the viaduct, houses and bushes

In later versions, the mountain became a more dominant element and completely fills the upper third of the painting. Perspective is defined only by the vertical and horizontal pattern of brush strokes in the foreground.

The brushstrokes are arranged in slabs of vibrant colour, in an almost abstract composition

Dense and vibrant blocks of colour have been used to buid up the structure of the mountain, sky, landscape and houses

The forerunner of modern art

Cézanne was rarely satisfied with his work. He signed only those paintings that he was completely happy with. When he died, many paintings were found rolled up in his studio. These had failed to meet the exacting standards he had set for himself. He recognised, however, that he was responsible for the beginning of a new era in art. He said: 'I have blazed a trail; others will follow.'

Paul Gauguin (1848–1903)

Paul Gauguin was a well-to-do stockbroker with a wife and five children. He spent his childhood in Peru and began painting in 1873, when he was working in Paris. As an amateur 'Sunday painter', he had come in contact with Corot and spent many weekends painting in the countryside.

Links with the Impressionists

- In 1877 he met with Pissarro and became involved with the Impressionists.
- This was to be a turning point in his life, and for the next six years or so he spent his holidays working with Pissarro at Pontoise.
- Under the influence of Pissarro, he turned to bright primary colours. Years later, Gauguin (who was not always generous to his fellow artists) admitted that Pissarro was the master from whom he had learned a great deal.
- Gauguin exhibited with the Impressionists at five of their shows, but the Impressionist artists were not all accepting of him.
- Monet and Renoir in particular disapproved of their shows being open to 'any dauber', but Degas seems to have admired Gauguin's work and even bought some of it.
- Gauguin's membership in the group was tolerated because of his friendship with Pissarro and also perhaps because of his wealth.
- He built up quite a collection of Impressionist paintings and particularly admired the work of Degas and Cézanne, in spite of Cézanne's acute dislike of him.
- In 1883 he resigned from his job and took his family to his wife's home in Copenhagen.
- He later returned to Paris and his painting career began to advance.

Pont Aven

- In 1886, Gauguin made his first visit to Pont Aven in Brittany, where he gathered a considerable following about him and was at last in the role of a master.
- Pont Aven was for him an escape from Paris and civilisation. He felt that the rural life was making him young again.
- In 1888 he spent some time with van Gogh in the South of France at Arles.
- This period turned out to be disastrous for both artists, and Gauguin returned to Paris.

- Gauguin was now becoming well known, and his painting had acquired a new and personal stamp thanks to the influence of Japanese prints and the work of Cézanne.
- Gauguin felt that it was important not to paint too closely from nature but to draw it out, to dream about it and think more of the creation that resulted from this.
- He reduced his shapes to flat areas surrounded by strong outlines, and used only the most dominating of nature's colours.
- Gauguin more or less did away with shadows, made very little use of linear perspective and suggested depth in his pictures mainly through blocking planes of colour.

Tahiti

- In the end, a desire for a more primitive life led him to travel to Tahiti. His finest work was produced here.
- He used the Tahitian people to work through the mystery of human existence, which fascinated him.
- His paintings have an exotic character that is never simply picturesque, but expresses deep feelings.
- He regarded the primitive life with nostalgia but was always aware that he could never be innocent enough to become part of this 'lost paradise'.
- This accounts for an element of melancholy in his work and strange titles, such as *Where Do We Come From? Who Are We? Where Are We Going?*
- His dealer in France, Ambroise Vollard, sent him a regular allowance. However, buyers proved unreliable and he fell deeply into debt.
- He was constantly in trouble with the colonial authorities, and his life in Tahiti was in many ways more difficult than his time in France. Amazingly, none of this turbulence shows in his cool, timeless and mysterious paintings.
- He was sentenced to jail for three months for libel but while on appeal he died suddenly of a heart attack in May 1903.

Tahitian Women

This was painted in 1891, shortly after Gauguin's arrival in Tahiti. It depicts two Tahitian women on the beach, and shows the bold colour and design that Gauguin discovered in primitive art, with its flat forms and vibrant colours.

The large figures fill the composition and are set against a high horizon line that divides the sand from the dark sea in the distance

Gauguin presents a view of the island of Tahiti as a serene and peaceful haven. One of the women is dressed in traditional fashion and the other is dressed in the Western style that would have been introduced by the missionaries.

Two Tahitian Women

The women of Tahiti, with their gentle, classic beauty, fascinated Gauguin and he painted them many times. This painting is one of the most beautiful of his Tahitian works.

Dressed in South Sea Island costume, the women represent Gauguin's dream of an idyllic society

They carry a basket of mango blossoms, the most typical flower of the tropics. It seems to represent an offering of their innocence and purity of spirit.

Where Do We Come From? Who Are We? Where Are We Going?

This was painted at a time of deep depression for the artist when his health was failing.

The painting reads from right to left. The sleeping infant asks 'Where do we come from?'

The crouching old woman asks 'Where are we going?'

The standing figure in the middle asks 'Who are we?' She stretches to pick the fruit from the tree, symbolising the pleasures of life. Behind her is a dark figure of an idol with arms outstretched; this is a reminder of the menace that always lurks around humanity.

Influence on Picasso

After Gauguin's death, an exhibition was held in the first Salon d'Automne in Paris in 1903. Another major retrospective in 1906 had a powerful influence on the French avant-garde (new and experimental artists) and in particular on Pablo Picasso. Gauguin's work led directly to Picasso's landmark painting of 1907: *Les Demoiselles d'Avignon*.

Vincent van Gogh (1853–90)

Van Gogh's painting career was one of the shortest but most intense in the history of art. He died at 37 years of age, only four years after he discovered his style and eight years after he began painting. He was brought up in rural Holland as the son of a Dutch minister and took up painting only after various failures in his life had driven him to despair. He was deeply affected by all the poverty around him and wanted to be a preacher, but his personality was not considered suitable.

Painting

Art soon became van Gogh's mission. His first paintings were of peasants and they show a deep concern and respect for the working life and its hardships. These early pictures are coarsely rendered and painted with rugged brushstrokes in dark, earthy tones.

He came to Paris in 1885 and saw the final Impressionist show. Van Gogh admired Paul Gauguin intensely and under his influence, he abandoned the dull muted colours in favour of pure bright colours. His brushstrokes also became more broken up.

Van Gogh's technique and style

Van Gogh used:

- Bright exaggerated colour that expressed emotion
- Energetic and whirling brush strokes
- Thick impasto paint to create raised almost three-dimensional surfaces.

Subjects

Van Gogh painted still life, landscape and portraits.

Arles and the South

Van Gogh went to the South of France, settling in Arles in the region of Provence. The architecture, landscape and people fed his imagination. Influenced by Japanese prints, he was thrilled with the sun and its brightness and saw it as 'being as beautiful as Japan'. He worked at a frenzied pace but his brushsrokes broadened, his drawing became more confident and his colours became brighter and stronger.

Gauguin

Van Gogh dreamed of starting an artists' colony in Arles and begged Gauguin to join him. The house he rented was painted yellow, his favourite colour, and this delighted him. He created a series of paintings in the 'Yellow House' in preparation for Gauguin's visit that he hoped would impress him.

Bedroom in Arles

The bedroom was simply painted in bright colours that he intended should be restful.

The picture welcomes the arrival of his friend to the house by including two of everything. Two pictures hang on the wall, there are two chairs and two pillows on the bed.

Composition

The artist has exaggerated the shape of the room and sharper perspective lines to include the bed, window and door. The three walls make the room seem small and enclosed, but this is balanced by the large area of floor that conveys a sense of space.

Vase with Twelve Sunflowers

Van Gogh painted several paintings of sunflowers in a vase as part of his preparations for Gauguin's visit. He treated the traditional subject of flowers in a vase in a simple and direct way.

Colour

The picture is painted mostly in ochres, yellows and gold, and the flowers are worked in short dabs of thick paint to suggest their seed heads

Composition

The line of the shallow foreground is picked up by the line on the curve of the vase

The asylum in St-Rémy

Gauguin's stay with van Gogh was a disaster and the artists quarrelled badly. During one of these quarrels van Gogh attacked Gauguin and later that evening cut off a piece of his own ear. Gauguin left and van Gogh suffered an increasing amount of breakdowns. He signed himself into a mental asylum at St-Rémy, a town near Arles, in April 1889. He spent one year there but it proved to be one of the most creative times in his life as an artist.

The Starry Night

Van Gogh painted the nearby landscape, but *The Starry Night* was painted from imagination. When he suffered bouts of depression he had a terrible need for religion and this led him to paint the stars.

Composition
The vertical shape of the cypress tree fills the left-hand side and balances the composition against the undulating blues and exploding yellows of the sky

The village is set in the lower part of the painting, nestling beneath the powerful energy of the whirling shapes. This rhythm is further accentuated by the thick brushstrokes and impasto paint used by the artist.

Self-Portrait

A self-portrait painted after van Gogh left the hospital at St-Rémy shows the artist was once again in a very disturbed state.

The deeply piercing eyes and, in particular, the deep frown in his forehead show his agitated state of mind

The ice blue swirling patterns of the background and the jacket contrast sharply with the fiery red hair and beard

Auvers and Dr Gachet

After his time in the South, van Gogh moved back to Paris where he settled in a café at Auvers under the watchful eye of Dr Gachet, a friend and patron of the arts. He worked as intensely as ever on canvases filled with wild swirling lines. However, he suffered from severe depression and on 27 July 1890 he shot himself in a cornfield while working at his easel. He died two days later, attended by his brother Theo and Dr Gachet.

Influence on Matisse and German Expressionism

Van Gogh became one of the most admired of all modern masters, but he sold only one painting in his lifetime. His Expressionist technique strongly influenced Henri Matisse (1869–1954) and his circle of Fauvist painters, as well as the German Expressionists.

2017 Ordinary Level paper: Section II, Question 12

Dance at Le Moulin de la Galette by Pierre Auguste Renoir (1841–1919) is illustrated on the accompanying sheet.

Answer (a) and (b).

(a) Describe and discuss this work using the following headings:

- Subject matter
- Composition
- Techniques and use of colour

(b) Briefly describe and discuss Impressionism.

Illustrate your answer.

Go to www.impressionniste.net, click English version and select an artist at the top of the page.

Visit www.khanacademy.org and search for 'Realism, Impressionism and Post-Impressionism'.

2016 Ordinary Level paper: Section II, Question 12

Choose one work that you have studied by Claude Monet (1840–1926).

Answer (a) and (b).

(a) Name, describe and discuss the work under the following headings:

- Subject matter
- Composition
- Style and use of colour

(b) Give some general information on Claude Monet.

Illustrate your answer.

Marking scheme

Q. 12		Marks	Notes
A	Name, description and discussion of chosen work	25	5 for name 20 for discussion
B	General information on Claude Monet	15	
C	Sketches	5	
	Total	50	

2015 Higher Level paper: Section II, Question 12

'Georges Seurat's (1859–1891) study of the scientific theories of colour is apparent in his distinctive style of painting.'

Discuss this statement with reference to *A Sunday Afternoon on the Island of La Grande Jatte* illustrated on the accompanying sheet and refer in your answer to subject matter, composition, style, technique, and influences.

and

Briefly describe and discuss one other named work by this artist.

Illustrate your answer.

Marking scheme

Q. 12		Marks	Notes
A	Discussion of statement	10	
B	Discussion of the painting illustrated referring to subject matter, composition, style/technique and influences	20	
C	Name and brief description and discussion of **one** other work by Seurat	15	5 for name 10 for description and discussion
D	Sketches	5	
	Total	50	

SAMPLE ANSWER

A Sunday Afternoon on the Island of La Grande Jatte by Georges Seurat was exhibited at the last Impressionist show in Paris 1886. It was the main attraction of the show and the amazing new style stunned the Parisian art world. It was immediately called 'Scientific Impressionism' by the press and an art critic Félix Fénéon was the first to use the term 'Neo-Impressionism'. He described the work of Seurat and his followers as a 'conscious and scientific' approach to the problems of colour and light.

Study of the scientific theories

Seurat had been influenced by the Impressionists, but he also became very interested in the latest scientific findings on the nature of colour by the French chemist Eugène Chevreul and the American physicist Ogden Rood. His studies of the two scientists' theories inspired him to challenge Impressionist ideas and move beyond their effort to capture the essence of a fleeting moment in time by painting with loose brushstrokes. He continued to paint landscape and social scenes out of doors but his experiments with colour led him to develop 'Pointillism', a new and distinctive style of painting.

Pointillism

Pointillism involved the separation of colour, or 'Divisionism', and the placing of hundreds of dots of pure complementary colours side by side. These specks of colour combined before the spectator's eyes in an optical illusion, as blue and red became purple, and natural colours mingled with complimentary colours like red with green and orange with blue. This changed the perception of colours completely, and created an amazing effect of reflected sunlight. This spectacular brightness of colour became the main attraction of this style, and it was immediately recognised as a new direction for modern painting.

A Sunday Afternoon on the Island of La Grande Jatte

La Grande Jatte was an island on the Seine. Seurat spent the mornings sketching there and painting in his studio in the afternoons. The giant canvas took him two years to complete.

Subject matter

This is an everyday scene of respectable, well-to-do Parisian people in fashionable dress enjoying their leisure. However, there is no sense of a naturalistic portrayal of real people. Many of the faces are not clear and there is no sense of movement or interaction amongst any of the groups or individuals.

Style

The painting is more in the style of an ancient Greek frieze. Seurat wanted to create that kind of solemn and still atmosphere. He carefully arranged the groups in what he called harmonies of colour.

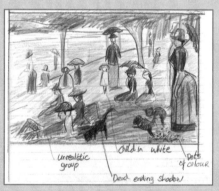

A Sunday Afternoon on the Island of La Grande Jatte sketch

These statuesque and dreamlike people face only sideways or straight ahead, and this adds to the frozen-in-time look and monumental quality of the painting. A man with a pipe, a woman with a book, and a moustached man with a cane and top hat are quite clearly together, and yet they appear psychologically isolated. The wet nurse, wearing an orange headscarf, is reduced to a geometric shape. In the foreground to the left, we see the separate classes of people – lower, middle and upper class – relaxing alongside each other, but in reality such a group would never have existed in that society.

The overall effect of the painting is more formal-looking than Impressionism and although the light is very bright, the shadows come to an immediate dead end in a sharp cut-off point.

Composition

The picture is carefully proportioned and balanced so that everything of interest is easily seen. The diagonal line of the water on the left creates an illusion of space, and the clearly defined areas of light and shade take the eye steadily back into the painting.

The river on the left balances the large figures of the fashionable couple on the right. In the foreground, three people are seen casually sitting down. In the centre middle ground, a woman is holding a small child. These three groups, isolated from one another, create a composition and the eye is immediately drawn to the young girl in white.

Bathers at Asnières

Unlike the fashionable Bourgeois people relaxing on the Island of La Grand Jatte, an earlier painting by Seurat, *Bathers at Asnières*, shows a group of working class men relaxing on the of riverbank of the opposite side.

The painting is vibrant and bright, and colours are placed together to create an overall unity. For example, the grass is made up of green, yellow and grey, and the young man's swimming shorts use orange, pink and blue with a little black, although it was not was not yet painted in the Pointillist technique. This is because the artist had not developed the method; instead, he dabbed on the paint and worked over it later with dots of contrasting colour.

Subject matter

The subject makes a subtle political point. Asnières was an industrial suburb on the River Seine, and factories in the background can be seen with smoke coming from one of the chimneys. In the middle of the river there is a ferry with a lady and a gentlemen sitting in the boat. We recognise them as people of leisure because she has a sunshade and he has a top hat, but the ferryman has to stand up to paddle them to the other side.

***Bathers at Asnières* sketch**

Composition

Diagonal lines means the eye is drawn first to the young man with a bright red hat sitting on the river bank, and then immediately to the paled-skinned boy standing in the water.

The end of Neo-Impressionism

Seurat's systematic, logical approach to painting did not last very long. The dot-by-dot technique was hard to work with and took too long, so the other artists lost interest soon after the artist's death at the early age of 31.

SAMPLE QUESTION

2017 Higher Level paper: Section II, Question 12

'Vincent van Gogh (1853–1890) was a Post-Impressionist artist whose work is best known for its vivid colour, striking brushwork and emotional impact.'

Discuss this statement with reference to one named work by Vincent van Gogh. In your answer refer to subject matter, composition, colour, style and techniques.

and

Briefly describe and discuss Vincent van Gogh's influence on twentieth-century art.

Illustrate your answer.

Break down the question

Statement: 'Vincent van Gogh's work is best known for its vivid colour, striking brushwork and emotional impact'

Task words

Discuss

Refer

Consider

Vivid colour

Striking brushwork

Emotional impact

Choose a painting and select expressive words to describe it like:

- Van Gogh's dramatic, imaginative, rhythmic and emotional technique and style.
- His impulsive, gestural application of paint and his use of colour to express emotion.

Consider

Subject matter – what is the painting about? What does it represent?

Composition – how are the art elements arranged and organised?

Colours – are they bright, vibrant, intense – primary colours?

Style – how has the artist approached the subject – is his way of working unique and recognisable?

Technique – what kind of brushstrokes does the artist use in the work – are they long and sweeping or are they short dabs and dashes? Is the paint thick and impasto?

SAMPLE ANSWER

Vincent van Gogh's *The Starry Night* is a masterful work of Expressionism and is often considered to be his greatest achievement. It epitomises that artist's impulsive, gestural application of paint, his use of vivid colour and his rhythmic and deeply expressive brushstrokes. The emotion is palpable in the swirling, tumultuous depiction of stars that explode like fireworks over the dark and forceful waves of sky that churn and pulsate with energy across the painting.

Unlike most of his works, this is a dramatic and imaginative work. It was painted from memory and it shows a radical departure from his previous, more naturalistic landscapes painted out of doors. It reflects the artist's own deep thoughts about the spirituality of man and nature.

The South of France

Born in Holland, Vincent van Gogh first came to Paris in 1885. Formal art training was too rigid for him but he met some of the Impressionists and learned a great deal from them. In Holland he had used a lot of dark browns and greys but in Paris he adopted the bright colours of the Impressionists and soon began to develop a unique style of his own.

He found city life too much of a strain so he left Paris and travelled to the South of France to the town of Arles in Provence. He was immediately captivated by the light and colours of the South and began working at a frenzied pace. As he worked, his strokes broadened, his drawing became more confident and his colours became stronger and brighter. He now applied paint in rhythmic dashes and thick impasto swirls that stood out from the canvas. His favourite colours were yellow, deep blue and emerald green, but he still liked to use some black and dark brown to create emphasis. He also used contrasting colours like red and green to express the full range of human passion.

Letters to Theo

Van Gogh always had tremendous support from his younger brother, Theo, who helped him in every possible way both emotionally and financially so that he could devote himself to his painting. Vincent wrote numerous letters to Theo, pouring out his feelings about his life and work. He told his brother that he was not satisfied to paint just what he saw. Instead he tried to express emotion using pure colour. He exaggerated what he considered important and dismissed that which he considered trivial or insignificant.

The Starry Night

The Starry Night was painted during a period spent in the asylum in St-Rémy in 1889 following a severe breakdown. Throughout his life, van Gogh had suffered from mental instability but this had become much worse over the years. After he had signed himself into the asylum he continued painting with the same furious intensity, producing numerous works in a very short time. He also wrote to Theo about his terrible need for religion. When he felt like this he said he wanted to paint the stars.

Subject matter

Van Gogh was greatly inspired by the rocky landscape in the countryside around St-Rémy and he includes a cypress tree, which is so characteristic of Provence in the painting. However, the distinctive church spire suggests the little village was inspired by his native Holland.

The Starry Night **sketch**

Composition

The composition is very strictly ordered to create balance and tension against the swirling movement of the cypress trees and the night sky. The tree seems to mimic the tower of the church and, flaring upwards on the left, it cuts sharply upwards like a flame through the foreground, middle ground and background in total contrast with the direction of the immense swirls of the sky. The gently sloping diagonal of the hills places the village in the lower end of the painting. This low horizon line helps to create depth.

Techniques and style

Writing to his brother, Van Gogh explained that the painting was a deliberate exercise in stylisation and that the arrangement was an exaggeration. He said the lines were contorted 'like those of ancient woodcuts'.

The long, sweeping and richly textured brushstrokes, and fluid, undulating blue and grey lines create rhythm, energy and emotion in the night sky. In contrast, the bright yellow of the swirling stars are painted briskly with dashes. The crescent moon at the top right-hand corner shines an even brighter yellow and orange, and van Gogh has outlined the distant buildings to distinguish them from the blue tones of the hills.

Influences

Van Gogh's distinctive style and use of bold and vibrant colours greatly influenced Fauvism, the first twentieth-century movement in modern art. The Fauves ('wild beasts') were a loosely allied group of French painters with shared interests, but van Gogh's 'self-expression' and search for a personal emotional truth also paved the way for Expressionism. He was greatly admired in Germany and artists Ernst Ludwig Kirchner and others of Die Brücke group of German Expressionists were fascinated by his brushwork and strongly contrasting bright colours.

Sketch of *Five Women on the Street* by Ernst Ludwig Kirchner

Unfortunately, the artist who so quickly became one of the most admired of all modern masters sold only one painting in his lifetime and had a short and sad life. At the age of 37, while suffering from deep depression when he was painting in a cornfield, he shot himself with a revolver and died a few days later.

SAMPLE QUESTION

'Edouard Manet (1832–1883) is often referred to as the father of Impressionism but his ambition had always been to be an Academic artist.'

Discuss this statement with reference to *Le Déjeuner sur l'herbe*, which is illustrated on the accompanying sheet. In your answer refer to subject matter, composition, colour, style and techniques used by the artist.

and

Name and briefly discuss one other work by this artist.

Illustrate your answer.

Marking scheme

Q.		Marks	Notes
A	Discussion of statement	10	
B	Discussion of the painting illustrated referring to subject matter, composition, colour, style and technique	20	
C	Name and brief description and discussion of **one** other work by Manet	15	5 for name 10 for description and discussion
D	Sketches	5	
	Total	50	

SAMPLE ANSWER

Édouard Manet is often described as an Impressionist but he was never part of the group. He supported and encouraged them and was very happy to play the part of modern master to these younger artists but, in 1874, when they put on an independent show, he steadfastly refused to take part. His new and ground-breaking style of painting greatly inspired artists like Monet, Renoir and Degas, and they looked up to him and learned from him, but Manet's own ambition had always been to be a successful established Academic artist. This never changed throughout his life.

He had trained in the studio of respected painter Thomas Couture and had the highest of regard for his teacher, but by the late nineteenth century the Academy of Fine Arts had become very rigid and their strict system of instruction frustrated him. He said: 'I paint what I see, and not what others choose to see.' He greatly admired seventeenth-century Dutch and Spanish painting and was very inspired by Venetian art. He had a clear vision of how he wanted to modernise these grand traditions in a specifically French way, and after he left Couture's studio he set out to develop his own ideas and style.

His goal was to show his work at the Salon, the huge annual fine arts exhibition in Paris, and to gain widespread recognition in this way. Unfortunately, the Academy had strict rules and expectations for painting, and because they had a strong influence on public opinion there was no other way artists could achieve success. Manet had no wish to go against this but his ideas did not fit with Academic thinking.

In the beginning, he had moderate success at the Salon but none of his paintings created the reaction he longed for. His great opportunity came in 1863 when his painting was rejected by the Salon. That year, so many paintings by other artists had also been refused that Emperor Napoleon III put pressure on the Salon committee and they set up a special Salon des Réfusés. The Salon des Réfusés, attracted more than 1,000 people a day, but most went out of curiosity or to laugh, jeer or even be shocked at the works the highly respected establishment had rejected. Manet's painting *Le Déjeuner sur l'herbe* caused an immediate outcry and deep outrage.

Le Déjeuner sur l'herbe

This became one of the most talked-about paintings at the exhibition, and the scandal turned Manet into a celebrity. However, art critics accused him of only trying to shock people.

The first upset to the establishment was that the artist had chosen a very large canvas and in the Academic tradition this was reserved for 'history painting' or subjects from

Sketch of *Le Déjeuner sur l'herbe*

mythology or religious stories that had an uplifting moral story or a pleasing non-controversial subject.

Subject matter

Originally called *Le Bain (The Bath)* nobody understood what Manet's highly controversial work was supposed to represent. It depicted a nude woman sitting on the ground having a picnic in the woods with two fully clothed men. In the background, a woman was bathing in the river, wearing only her undergarments. Another insult as far as the establishment was concerned was that the work was based on *Fête Champêtre*, a well-known and loved painting in the Louvre by the sixteeth-century Venetian artist, Giorgione.

Manet's model was Victorine Meurant; she was well known in artistic circles, but this modern woman's direct, cool gaze was far more sensual than any remote ancient goddess. The fruit spilling from the basket nearby and the discarded clothing on the ground beside her added even more to this explicitly erotic image.

Composition

The viewers also found the composition extremely confusing. The foreground lighting was directly on the subject as if it had come from a studio window, but the lighting in the background fell straight down from above like sunlight. The woodland scene was painted with thin, loose brushstrokes but the figures and trees in the foreground looked more real and finished. This clearly gave the impression that the girl was painted from life but the bather in the background and her surroundings were from a painting. In other words, it was a painting within a painting but nobody knew what the artist meant by this.

Colour

Manet went against Academic painting techniques in several key ways. He placed colours side by side on the canvas rather than mixing them carefully on the palette. This is called 'optical mixing', which means the colours mix before the eyes of the viewer. He chose different colours to suggest tone and used stark contrasts of light and dark instead of grading the tone. This meant the figures tended to 'flatten out' rather than have the traditional smooth, rounded finish.

Style and technique used by the artist

He liked to work quickly using loose brushstrokes, and instead of slowly building up colours with oily glazes he used quite thick paint, applied wet paint on wet and even left parts of the canvas uncovered. This made the surface quite rough and the Academy had a strong preference for a smooth, enamel-like surface and fully blended colours and brushstrokes.

An agreeable character

After the scandal of Le Déjeuner sur l'herbe, the popular idea was that Manet was a rough, almost revolutionary type, but he was far from that. He was a man of great charm, wit and elegance, and even the critics had to admit that he was a most 'agreeable character' and commented on his 'correct appearance'. He came from a wealthy, privileged background, had a very wide circle of friends, and had many supporters in literary and artistic communities. These supporters included the Impressionist painters; every week Claude Monet and other artists joined him in the Café Guerbois, near his studio, to discuss art.

Manet was also influenced by the Impressionists. The artists encouraged him to paint out of doors and, as a result, his painting became lighter in tone. They also persuaded him to use colour in shadow instead of grey or black and to observe the effect of light on water.

However, he never wavered from his ambition to achieve official recognition; for 20 years the Salon remained his battleground. He worked relentlessly on major compositions that he hoped would be successful, but he suffered rejection after rejection. Fortunately, he never had any money problems because he inherited his father's fortune in 1862 but he suffered deeply all his life when his work was mocked and ridiculed. Success came eventually but it was too late for him.

A Bar at the Folies-Bergère

In 1882, *A Bar at the Folies-Bergère* was accepted by the Paris Salon and exhibited there to great acclaim from critics and audiences. However, it was to be Manet's last great painting. The stage entertainment at the Folies-Bergère attracted a wide audience that included prostitutes and men of all classes looking for casual relationships. Manet knew the place well. He made a number of preparatory sketches there but the final work was painted in his studio. He set up a bar and asked one of the barmaids, Suzon, to be as his model.

Sketch of *A Bar at the Folies-Bergère*

A huge mirror behind the main figure reflects the massive crowd, but this device is used by the artist to trick our visual perceptions. We realise the young woman's reflection does not match her figure, and a man is standing directly in front of her but his reflection is also off to the side. Resting her hands firmly on the bar counter, she stares out blankly and with no sign of emotion. She dominates the central position and holds our gaze, but the blurred Impressionist-like background creates the sense of people moving about. Her dress as well as the other solid realities in the foreground like the bowl of fruit and the bottles have been rendered with meticulous realism. Manet won a medal for this painting at the Salon but unfortunately he did not live long enough to enjoy it. He died in in April of 1883, aged 51. *A Bar at the Folies-Bergère* is considered one of the greatest masterpieces of the nineteenth century.

C. Fitton, 2017

Twentieth-century art movements

Fauvism

Fauvism was not an art movement as such, and the group had no theory or strong philosophical ideas. They were bound together more by the vision of Henri Matisse, the landscapes of the South of France and a shared love of colour.

The artists

- The artists' approach varied quite considerably, although the main influence on the group was Gauguin.
- Henri Matisse was a master of colour and he constantly explored its potential. He used vivid colour and bold patterns to express his concept of an ideal world.
- Maurice de Vlaminck was deeply impressed by van Gogh and painted in strong, bright colours, particularly red.
- André Derain used pure colour, outlining, as Gauguin had done, in blue. He sectioned the colours into separate compartments in a method known as Cloisonnism.

Unusual colour harmonies

- The Fauves looked for unusual colour harmonies and rejected the traditional method of light and shade in favour of shapes constructed only with line and colour.
- They considered painting as first and foremost a flat surface to be covered with colour assembled in a certain order.
- Like van Gogh and Gauguin, they felt that colour should bring out feelings and sensations.

The end of Fauvism

The movement lasted only three years. It came to an abrupt end when Henri Matisse became dissatisfied with its crudeness and lack of discipline. In 1908 the artists went their separate ways and Matisse embarked on a highly productive career. This earned him a revered place in twentieth-century art history, second only to Picasso, his great rival artist.

Henri Matisse (1869–1954)

- Matisse was introduced to the work of the Impressionists and van Gogh early in his career. Cézanne's work had the greatest impression on him.
- In the midst of mounting misfortune and continuous derision from critics (and even his own father), Henri Matisse came close to abandoning painting for good. However, he weathered each storm and kept creating new works, all of which he chose to paint with his distinct modernistic approach.
- After the exhibition of 1905, the group acquired the title 'Les Fauves', but Matisse never liked this. He was acutely aware of the complex problems produced by the movement and knew that random application of bright colours was not enough.

- He set out to prove that colour did not need modelling, perspective or the traditional light and shade. He argued that pure colour could create volume and space that would not take away from the richness of the picture.

The South

The South of France was a source of great inspiration to Matisse. In 1905, he went to Collioure to work with André Derain. His wife was the model for his work, which was painted in strong and vibrant colour. This caused a huge shock shock to the viewers of the Autumn Exhibition.

Pattern

Matisse was also captivated by the sculpture of Africa and Islamic art, and he loved pattern in all kinds of fabrics.

Hotel windows

In 1917, he moved more or less permanently to the South of France to an apartment in the Hotel Regina situated above the town of Nice. He painted many scenes through the window. These works convey an image of the outside world from a position of comfort and security.

A successful career

Matisse became very successful in the 1930s but in 1941, after an operation for cancer, he was confined to a wheelchair. He continued to expand his work and experimented more with line drawing and illustrating poems.

Cut-out shapes

In his last years he relied greatly on cut-out shapes, which he applied directly onto the canvas or pinned to the wall. His work was shown in a large retrospective exhibition in the Museum of Modern Art in New York in 1951. He died in 1954.

Portrait of Madame Matisse. The Green Line

The model is Matisse's wife, Amelie, and the painting was shown at the Autumn Exhibition of 1905. Matisse bypassed the traditional method of light and shade and replaced it with areas of flat colour in strong contrasting tones.

Viewers at the Autumn Exhibition found the use of strong unnatural colours difficult to accept in the human figure

The Dessert: Harmony in Red

The red room is dominated by the colour red, but it is also a celebration of pattern and decoration inspired by oriental art.

The decorative blue floral pattern on the tablecloth and wallpaper is picked up in the background and on the trees seen through the window. This links the interior with the cooler green exterior and takes the eye deep into the depths of the painting.

Despite the flat colours, the artist has managed to create an impression of space, and the figure in a white apron arranging fruit in a dish looks quite natural and can move with ease.

Cubism

- Pablo Picasso and Georges Braque worked in Paris between 1907 and 1914. Together they developed Cubism, which was to become one of the most influential art styles of the early twentieth century.
- The word itself came about after a French art critic Louis Vauxcelles saw some landscapes painted by Braque which had in turn been influenced by Cézanne. Picasso's ground-breaking *Les Demoiselles d'Avignon*, painted in 1907, was also highly influential on the development of the style. The flattening-out of space and the breaking up of the shallow background in this painting became the characteristic features of Cubism.
- Georges Braque (1882–1963) began as a Fauve artist but changed direction. In 1907 he began to work with Picasso, and together they broke with the Renaissance system of perspective.
- They were influenced by Cézanne's manner of breaking space into interwoven planes of colour, and they based their efforts on his famous remark that 'one must detect in nature the sphere, the cone and the cylinder'.

Characteristics of Cubism

The artists painted everyday objects like bottles, glasses, pipes, newspapers, guitars, violins and even the human figure, but changed them by:

- Fragmenting and bringing them almost to the point where they no longer existed (in other words 'abstract art') but did not quite cross that threshold.
- Painting 'as one thinks things, not as one sees them' (Picasso).

- Putting the thought process or 'conception' in artwork before imitation or the representation of reality.
- Making the work of art a reality or a 'pictorial fact' (Braque).

Reality in Cubism

Painting became more about itself and not what it represented, but Cubism was never a rejection of reality. According to Cubist theory, a closer knowledge of nature required new methods of representing it. The artists' theory was that the eye is always moving and constantly changing, shifting its range of vision to reconstruct distances, surfaces and volumes.

Collage

Picasso was the first artist to use collage or something other than paint on the surface of the canvas. He and Braque then continued to use paper, cloth and other textured materials in their paintings.

Pablo Picasso (1881–1973)

Picasso was not, in fact, the most revolutionary artist of the twentieth century, but his name stood for everything that was daring, aggressive and extravagant. He turned convention upside down, bewildering the public with unexpected and sensational innovations that earned him the reputation of an outrageous modern artist.

Blue Period

He first came to Paris in 1900 and within a year he was painting in cold blue tones. He painted young, sad, bloodless women, sickly children and old and emaciated beggars.

Rose Period

Three years later he painted harlequins, acrobats and itinerant circus folk in pinks or 'rose' colours. The figures were still solemn and unsmiling, but did not look quite as mournful and depressed as in the previous period.

Cubism

- In 1907 Picasso began to work with Georges Braque and developed the first ideas of Cubism. Cézanne influenced him considerably, but he had been very impressed by African art which he saw in 1907 in the ethnographic museum in Paris.
- Influenced by African masks, he painted *Les Demoiselles d'Avignon*, one of the most powerful paintings of the century. Picasso worked closely with Braque at this time, and for a while their work was almost indistinguishable from each other. Braque, however, worked slowly and deliberately, while Picasso was always in a hurry.

Working alone

- After Braque was seriously wounded in the First World War, Picasso painted alone. In 1917 he went to Rome to design sets for the famous Russian Ballet company and married one of the dancers dancer named Olga Khokova. He made some very fine line drawings of Olga and was inspired by his Italian experience to paint female nudes in the Neoclassical tradition of Ingres.

- Between 1920 and 1924, Picasso painted his last Cubist works. Two great compositions from this time are entitled *Three Musicians*. Picasso's work changed as he searched continuously for a way to express himself with complete freedom. However, he watched the oncoming tide of the war in the 1930s with great sorrow.

The South of France

Picasso remained in Paris during the German occupation and then moved to the South of France. He remained a figure of huge popular acclaim with almost the stature of a film star throughout his career as an artist. Until his death in 1973, Picasso painted, sculpted and experimented unceasingly.

Les Demoiselles d'Avignon

Picasso set the scene of Cubism with this ground-breaking painting in which he fuses several viewpoints at one time. The figures are stylised with limbs that are almost dislocated. It also broke new ground in its brutal sexual frankness. The women staring so directly at the viewer are prostitutes and are distinctly disturbing. This makes sense when we take Picasso's great fear of sexually transmitted disease into account.

The human figure
The women's faces are distorted and the features are wrenched out of line with one another. The source for this was Picasso's collection of African masks. The energy and distortion in African art greatly appealed to him.

Composition
The figures are tightly grouped together, and the eye is drawn from face to face in a rounded movement

The women's fixed stony gazes carry an air of menacing threat, and even the melon in the foreground looks like a sharp weapon

Three Musicians

The figures are all from the theatre and were inspired by ballet set and costume designs.

The colours are flat and brilliant. One of the artistist's favourite figures, the harlequin, sits on the left. The costume with its geometric possibilities fitted the style of Cubism perfectly.

Pierrot in his white costume sits in the middle

A monk sits on the right

The Spanish Civil War

The Spanish Civil War greatly upset Picasso, and the violence and emotion in his work reflected this. It moved him from his preoccupation with his own artistic and personal problems to depicting the terrible tragedy. The fate of the little Basque town of Guernica caused him to paint one of his most poignant works. Its message

key point

General Franco, dictator of Spain, asked that *Guernica* should be exhibited in Spain. Picasso relentlessly refused and it remained in New York for many years as the centrepiece of the collection in the Museum of Modern Art. In accordance with Picasso's will, they reluctantly returned it to Spain in 1981, following that country's return to a democratic government.

is a unique documentation of the horror and despair of the event, and is one of the most powerful denunciations of war ever depicted in modern art.

Guernica

In one of the most brutal acts of war ever perpetrated, the town of Guernica in the Basque region of Northern Spain was razed by German Fascist bombers who were supporters of General Franco. Picasso painted this huge work in just over a month for the Spanish Pavilion in the 1937 World Fair. The media was always important to the artist, and the giant painting has the black and white appearance of a screaming newspaper headline. With its combination of Surrealist and Cubist imagery in figures and beasts, it hit just the right note for the mood of the time and touched people's consciences.

The perpetrators are not shown but their presence is everywhere. Five figures express surprise, horror, grief, anger and despair, while two animals convey the sheer brutality of the act. The screaming wounded horse at the centre is one of the most important, largest and moving figures. This contrasts with an image of brute force in the figure of the bull.

A figure, reduced to the simplicity of a face and arm, stretches out of the window to light the scene with the lamp fo freedom. She discovers with dazed horror the spectacle of death and destruction.

A woman throws her arms to the sky as she and the house are in flames

A woman raises her head to the sky and cries out in a scream of pain over the body of her dead child

The fallen warrior lies between the horse's hooves. In his hand is a broken sword, and a flower grows from his clenched fist.

A woman runs from her house and seems to cry out not only for the tragedy of the town but for all humanity

SECTION 3

General Appreciation

- Topics vary considerably in this section of the exam, so it can be tricky to prepare for.
- Choose one or two areas of research from the list on the following pages.
- There is no guarantee that the topic you prepare will appear on the exam paper. Be flexible – be prepared to answer another question should this happen.
- If there is a study area of particular interest to you (e.g. film) there may be a question that will suit – if not, be ready to choose another.
- The original purpose of this section of the exam was to create an opportunity for you to discuss topics based on everyday visual experience in your own environment. You are not expected to be an expert in your chosen study area. Remember that in some general areas such as the environment, packaging, design, etc., your opinion is as good as the next. So be confident and express yourself well!

- To develop a critical awareness of a range of artworks by visiting museums and galleries
- To develop a critical awareness of public art in Ireland by visiting and examining individual works
- To consider the relationship between public art and architecture
- To develop the skills to describe, discuss, analyse and contrast design of objects and architectural artefacts
- To develop confidence in individual preferences for differing styles and tastes
- To develop awareness of the aesthetic elements in film
- To read film reviews
- To have an awareness of film as a form of visual communication
- To acquire an understanding of filming techniques by researching a range of popular films in magazines or online

Study areas

Museum and gallery studies

Gallery visits are fundamental to all aspects of the art syllabus. It is therefore vital to do the following:

A visit to a museum is the most common answer given, so yours needs to be special! Answer with enthusiasm. If you enjoyed the visit and found it special, then communicate that. If the visit helped your work in the classroom, explain this for the examiner.

- Visit an art gallery, art exhibition, museum or heritage centre.
- Read exhibition catalogues and other information relating to the visit.
- Find a website related to the gallery, museum or heritage centre.
- Examine the layout, lighting and labelling system of your chosen museum, gallery or heritage centre.
- Be informed about the history of the building and its location.
- Read reviews of exhibitions.
- Form your own opinions.

Film studies

To broaden your understanding of this study area, it is crucial to:

- Watch many films.
- Do some online research for background information on films.
- Watch the 'making of' features on YouTube.
- Research specific contemporary films.
- Research specific animated films.
- Gain knowledge of film-making techniques.
- Learn about animation techniques.
- Understand special effects.
- Study named film directors and their unique styles.
- Read reviews in newspapers and online.

Local public sculpture

- Research public sculpture in your locality.
- Find out the name of the artist.
- Find further examples of this artist's work.
- Research examples of public sculpture in other localities.

- Examine sculptures on motorways and roads, as well as parks, streets and squares in towns and cities.
- Read reviews and media features on public sculptures.

The built environment

- Gain knowledge of architecture. Learn the names of new buildings and research the architects who designed them.
- Be aware of town planning: streets, squares, shopfronts, etc. Pay particular attention to new or redesigned towns.
- Examine the buildings and streets in your area and inform yourself of its history and design.
- Read newspaper or magazine articles on architecture and town planning.

Graphic design, interior design and product design

General information and art terms from Practical Art class or Home Economics class may be useful to you here.

General topics

Appreciation is intended to test a general knowledge of art and aesthetics, so why not try answering a very general question? Most exam papers will feature one such general question.

A visit to an exhibition

This is one of the most popular questions on the Appreciation section. This is very understandable because visiting galleries and an art exhibition is a very interesting and rewarding experience. Take the time on your visit to examine the work, make notes and read reviews on the newspapers or online before and after. If you have a guide you will be told directly what to look for, but ask questions on anything you would like to know more about. Catalogues, leaflets and online reviews will also help you to engage with the work more fully. Communicate your informed but individual response in your answer. Be enthusiastic, and remember – your opinions matter!

key point

Do not make negative comments about the work. If you didn't like something, say why in a constructive way.

2017 Higher Level paper: Section II, Question 20

'Street art has become popular in Ireland in recent years with cities and towns embracing the exciting potential of the urban landscape.'

Discuss this statement with reference to the illustration on the accompanying sheet. In your answer refer to subject matter, composition, location and scale.

and

Briefly outline your visual concepts for a mural in your own locality.

Illustrate your answer.

TIPS FOR ANSWERING AN APPRECIATION QUESTION

- Write an interesting, descriptive essay putting forward your own reasons as to why you think street art has become so popular.
- Address each of the specific elements, subject matter, composition, location and scale listed in the question.
- Make your points with confidence, enthusiasm and even a bit of humour. Try to keep your examiner engaged!
- If your ideas are good, you will pick up very easy marks.
- The ideas for a mural are entirely up to you and involve mostly drawing and colour. This makes it a lovely question for young artists. Go for it!

All of the following questions are also open to individual opinion. Yours is just as interesting as the next. Use your everyday experience and studies in art to inform your answers.

SAMPLE EXAM QUESTIONS (2017, HIGHER LEVEL)

Q.17: 'Public sculpture plays an important role in commemorating people and/or events.'

Discuss this statement with reference to a named public sculpture you have studied. In your answer refer to subject matter, composition, materials, techniques, location and the context of the work.

and

Briefly outline your visual concepts for a public sculpture to be placed in your locality to commemorate a person or an event.

Illustrate your answer.

Q.18: 'The purpose of graphic design is to attract attention and communicate information.'

Discuss this statement with reference to the posters illustrated on the accompanying sheet. In your answer refer to imagery, layout, typography, colour and briefly outline which poster is more effective.

and

Briefly outline your visual concepts for a poster based on a festival of your choice.

Illustrate your answer.

Q.19: 'Product design should involve a balance between appearance and function.'

Discuss this statement with reference to the vacuum cleaner illustrated on the accompanying sheet. In your answer refer to form, function, materials and decorative qualities.

and

Briefly outline your visual concepts for a container/bag to carry your school lunch.

Illustrate your answer.

(To see the 2017 exam paper with the accompanying illustrations, go to www.examinations.ie, click on 'Examination Material Archive', on the left-hand side of the page, and then click on 'Examination Papers')

Answering a question on a visit to an exhibition or gallery

Questions relating to a visit to an art gallery or an art exhibition feature regularly on the Appreciation section of the Leaving Certificate Art examination paper. The question is likely to ask you to discuss **at least two** of the works in detail, but it may also focus on aspects like:

- the architecture of the gallery or museum building
- the curation and layout of the exhibition
- the display and lighting.

The building

Many art galleries were built for other purposes and have been altered to house the artworks. Some have had modern extensions or have been renovated to suit the display of art. This often enhances the atmosphere and helps with the enjoyment of art. Comparisons of the works shown in an older building with those shown in purpose-built extensions can be very interesting. Facilities like shops, restaurants, cloakrooms and lifts should also be noted.

Discuss

- What is the name of the art gallery and what city is it in?
- Was this building designed as an art gallery or for another purpose?
- Is this a modern or an old building?
- What are the main architectural features?
- How did you access the building?
- What atmosphere does the interior convey?

Layout of the exhibition

The layout of the exhibition is crucial to the enjoyment of the art. How sculpture is placed and how paintings are hung affects how we look at them. Often exhibitions are organised by a specific theme or in chronological order. Visitors should see the artworks at their ease, so seats are often provided so that they can rest and enjoy looking at the works.

Discuss

- How many rooms were in the exhibition? Were they easy to find?
- Was there information about the exhibition themes and the different artists?
- In your opinion, do you think there were too many or too few paintings on the walls?
- What types of artworks were there at the exhibition and were they all easy to find?

The curator

A curator is the keeper of the museum or the collection of artworks, but they may also be appointed to manage a particular exhibition. Working with other members of staff, a curator will make decisions on what works to select and how to display them.

Display of the artwork (lighting, design and layout)

Display refers to the practical aspects of arranging an exhibition, e.g. the space (where it is held), the lighting and the layout. The way in which the artworks are displayed must be considered very carefully.

Placement

Artworks are often hung from the midpoint of each painting so everyone can see them. The midpoint of each painting is usually about 60 inches or 154cms from the floor.

Colour on the wall

The walls are often coloured in bright blues, greens or even reds, but if these colours are complimentary to the works they will not distract. Take particular note because it is often hard to remember the colour of the wall when one is focusing on the art hanging or standing in front.

Labels

Labels are located to the side of the artwork with basic information regarding the artist, the title of the artwork, the medium of the work and its size.

Light

Lighting should be bright enough to see the work, but not so bright that there is a glare or difficulty in seeing the artworks. Strong lights can cause drawings, prints and watercolours to fade, so care has to be taken with light levels. Many exhibitions use a combination of natural and artificial light.

Frame

The frame of an artwork is also taken into consideration when hanging, and some paintings require glass to protect them. There are often barriers to protect the artworks, but these are normally not a distraction and create a comfortable distance between the visitor and the artwork.

Discuss

- Do you think the colour on the walls was distracting or made the artworks look better?
- Did the artworks have labels? What side were they on and why do you think they were placed there?
- Was the lighting too bright or too dim? What kind of lights were there?

The works of art

Looking and evaluating the artworks will help you understand and appreciate them better. Four of the easiest ways to approach this are to:

1. Look
2. Describe
3. Interpret
4. Research

1. Look

Look carefully at the work, paying close attention to details. Take a few moments to think: can you remember what you noticed? Now look back again.

- What details do you now see that you overlooked the first time?

2. Describe

Notice the formal elements of the painting or sculpture. The formal elements are:

- Subject matter, line, shape, colour, composition and materials.

Some of these elements are present in any work of art and will be organised according to the principles of design. This makes the artwork satisfying and pleasing to the eye. Try to find which ones are used in the work and how they are organised.

Subject

- What is the painting about or what does the sculpture represent? What do you see?

Composition

- How have the different art elements in the artwork been put together? What way is your eye drawn? Can you see shapes like triangles, diagonals and verticals?

Texture and brushstrokes

- How has the artist treated the surface or what is the texture of the work?
- If it's a sculpture is it free-standing or relief?
- Has colour been used to convey mood or atmosphere?

3. Interpret

The work of art may have a meaning or a message. The artist may use subtle ways to draw our attention to this. It might also refer to a subject that is well known to the viewer – for example, a religious work of art that was intended to be shared with a community who would have known the subject matter very well.

- Does the work convey a message or is the meaning hidden?
- Where is the painting set?
- Is there a narrative or story in the painting or sculpture?
- Does the work convey atmosphere? What emotion do you feel? Do you think the artist intended you to feel like this?

4. Research

Finding out more about the artist and the period during which they lived can greatly help you to appreciate their art. It can also help you to understand more about the work and why the artist chose the subject or worked in this style.

- In what period of history did this artist live?
- Was this produced as a religious work or was it created for a particular person? Was it perhaps a response to an event?
- Do you think the artist's social or historical background influenced the subject, style or technique in this work?
- What else do you know about the artist and their work?

Evaluate

At the end of the visit, take time to think about the works of art you have seen and how they were displayed.

- What aspects of the exhibition did you like best?
- Why did you like this?
- If you had curated this exhibition, is there anything you would have arranged differently?

Create

1. Make a series of sketches of your favourite artworks from the exhibition.

2. Sketch the layout of the exhibition, or part of it. Include as much detail as you can, such as the position of the sculpture or paintings, lights, doors and benches. Include the colour of the walls and labels. Pay attention to the different sizes of the artworks and how they were displayed.

SAMPLE QUESTION

2016 Higher Level paper: Section II, Question 16

'Architecture, floor plan, lighting and display techniques all influence the overall visitor experience and appreciation of works of art in a gallery or museum.'

Discuss this statement with reference to a named gallery or museum you have visited. Describe in detail two named works you found interesting and discuss how these works were displayed.

and

In your opinion, briefly outline two initiatives that would encourage young people to engage with works of art on display in museums or galleries.

Illustrate your answer.

Marking scheme

Q. 16		Marks	Notes
A	Discussion of statement and name of gallery or museum	15	10 for discussion of statement 5 for named gallery/museum
B	Detailed description of two named works, discussion of why they were interesting and how they were displayed	15	5 for named works (3/2) 5 for why interesting 5 for how displayed
C	Brief outline of two initiatives that would encourage young people to engage with works on display in museums and galleries	15	2 initiatives and information
D	Sketches	10	
	Total	50	

SAMPLE ANSWER

A visit to an exhibition

This year I visited two exhibitions in Ireland. I had the pleasure of visiting Dublin Castle to see an exhibition called 'Crawford at the Castle' with my aunt just before Christmas and later in the year I visited the Crawford Gallery in Cork with my Art class to visit to see the same exhibition called 'Crawford at the Castle, a Homecoming'.

> A question on a visit to an art gallery will sometimes give you an opportunity to discuss something special. See below how this student managed to compare two gallery visits.

The exhibition featured major works of Irish art from the permanent collection of the Crawford Art Gallery, Cork. This had travelled to Dublin for the first time in its almost 200-year-old history, and the 59 works were exhibited in both the historic State Apartments and the Coach House. They were exhibited again in April when the famous works came back home.

The layout of an exhibition is crucial, because the way paintings are hung really affects how we look at them. 'Crawford at the Castle' was curated by Anne Boddaert and Dr Michael Waldron, and I found it a most pleasant and engaging experience. I loved the setting and this helped me to really appreciated the works on display.

This is especially interesting because when I saw this exhibition again in Cork I found it a completely different experience. It was planned and curated by the same people but I was far less impressed and I found the works of art less appealing.

Architecture

The architecture of Dublin Castle probably had the most impact, and perhaps because of the Christmas atmosphere this exhibition left a more lasting impression on me. That December morning, we crossed the cobbled upper castle yard and when we stepped in from the cold we immediately felt at home in the warm and welcoming hallway of the State Apartments with its black and white tiling. There was wheelchair access, which is a vital facility in any public building, but once we got our tickets and put our coats in the cloakroom we headed towards the Grand Staircase with the large Christmas tree standing at the windows above.

This really set the scene for us, and walking up we imagined how it must have been for members of the aristocracy in the past who would have ascended this staircase in their elegant clothes to attend balls given by the Viceroy of Ireland. This is also the ceremonial route used during the inauguration ceremonies for the President of Ireland.

THE GRAND STAIRCASE DublinCastle

Sketch of the Grand Staircase in Dublin Castle

Floor plan

A floor plan would of course be very important in a large gallery with lots of rooms, but this was a small exhibition so we had no need for one. The long and magnificent corridor brought us straight to the exhibition in the State Apartments Galleries and perhaps because it was so near to Christmas there were very few visitors, so we had total freedom to enjoy the painting in such beautiful surroundings. The four rooms used as gallery spaces were originally the quarters of the Viceroy and his family, and they complimented the older paintings beautifully.

Lighting

The lighting was perfect. It was bright enough to see the work, but not so bright that there was a glare or difficulty in seeing them. Little spotlights hanging from a railing all around the ceiling subtly picked up each of the paintings and created a beautiful glow in the room.

Display techniques

Display techniques are very important in an exhibition, and the walls of the State Gallery rooms were painted either cobalt blue, ox blood or grey and this really made the artworks stand out.

The King's Room was my favourite. Many of the Crawford paintings are framed in gold and this looked fantastic against the beautiful blue walls. The paintings also blended in perfectly with the old-style décor. One of the most loved paintings from the Crawford collection, *The Red Rose* by John Lavery, was displayed over the fireplace. This made it easily the most dramatic work in the exhibition because the beautiful painting in reds and purples of Hazel, the artist's wife, looked as if it belonged there. It made the room more like a grand home instead of a gallery, and next to it in the alcove was a portrait of a lady at a large rounded Georgian window. This echoed the two large actual windows of the room and seemed to open a new 'space' in the corner.

The paintings were hung from the midpoint so everyone could see them – this midpoint was about one and a half metres from the floor. Large information panels on the walls were easy to see and read quickly. They gave us general information about the work and I found them very interesting and informative. I learned lots about the background and the labels on the wall to the left of the paintings were also very helpful.

Sketch of the King's Room in Dublin Castle

Paintings

Seán Keating's *Men of the South* and Barrie Cooke's *The Lough Derg Pike* were the two paintings that I found most interesting. *Men of the South* is a very large oil painting on canvas and this was displayed in the King's Room at right angles to the fireplace on a wall by itself. I was absolutely captivated by the subject matter, and the sepia-like browns and greens of the men's clothing and background looked amazing against the blue.

The scene shows an IRA flying column in about 1921 waiting in the Irish landscape in advance of an ambush of a passing British military control. However, I was intrigued to learn that in reality the men were all members of the north Cork brigade. Keating brought them into his studio to pose, but he changed their looks slightly to conceal their identity. I found out from reading the information that the artist himself was a staunch Republican and this certainly can be seen in the painting. It shows none of the grime and pain of war, only the patriotism. Holding their guns ready, the men are depicted as heroes with eyes fixed on their target, showing no thought of their own safety.

Sketch of *Men of the South* on display

The composition shows the influence of photography as the figures are cut off at the edges. All are shown in profile from a close point of view, and our eyes quickly follow their gaze from the standing figures on the left to those sitting on the lower right. This sharp diagonal is balanced by a figure standing behind them in the shadow of a bush.

The Lough Derg Pike by Barrie Cooke was my other favourite painting. This stood out because of its fabulous colours and large size, but in fact I never noticed it when I visited Dublin Castle. I only became aware of it in the 'Crawford at the Castle, a Homecoming' exhibition and that really surprised me because I found the exhibition in Cork quite disappointing compared to Dublin. It was held downstairs in the modern wing of the gallery and I felt most of the work that looked so beautiful in the elegant period rooms of Dublin Castle was lost in the stark plain setting. I thought it took away from the overall theme, and the light grey walls gave off a cold feeling that affected my enjoyment of the paintings.

However, *The Lough Derg Pike* looked great in the modern setting. It immediately caught my eye because the beautiful greens, turquoises and blues of the fish are painted over with gold in places to make it shine out from the blues of the background. This worked really well on the grey wall and I made a sketch on the spot. I was really interested to learn that Cooke himself has a great interest in marine life and that this is a life-sized depiction of a five-foot pike found many years ago in the waters of Lough Derg in County Clare. The real fish is apparently preserved in a pub there.

The fish is almost three-dimensional, standing well out from background. Below this the words 'THE LOUGH DERG PIKE' are written in large gold writing. A panel at the end contains mementos from the time it was caught, including a fishing rod. The artist was also inspired by the quotation from Heraclitus:

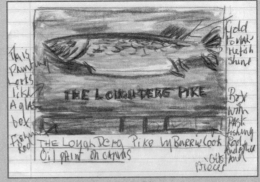

Sketch of *The Lough Derg Pike*

'All existence flows in the stream of creation and passing away.' He related this to the idea of living on a rainswept island that is traversed by rivers and the sport of fishing, that appears so often in Irish myths and legends.

Initiatives for young people

In my opinion, something that would encourage younger students to engage with works of art displayed in galleries would be through the process of sketching the paintings. A small booklet could be provided, in which they must draw a sketch of their favourite painting. After the visit, the young people could gather together to discuss the works in relation to the experience of making the sketch. They would have to say why they liked this work the best and I think they would learn art terms and correct language without realising it. This would help them to appreciate art better.

Another idea I would have is for slightly older students. Following a short talk after they arrive at the gallery, they would be divided into small groups. Each group would be given a certain amount of time in the gallery and they would each have different tasks. They might have to find out a small number of specific facts about the style of the paintings or the architecture, find out important background information or draw comparisons and make links between certain aspects of the work.

Their findings would all be shared when the groups come together at the end of the visit, and each group would allocate a spokesperson to talk about this. The reason I think this would work is because each group would want to be the best and that would make them really look at the works on display and work hard to find the correct information.

R. O'Driscoll, 2017